CAREERS IN FINANCE

Introduction

The book *Careers in Finance* has been prepared by the Financial Management Association International to assist college-level students of finance and business in evaluating alternate career paths and in linking their educational experience to their career aspirations. Specifically, *Careers in Finance* is designed to provide information on what professionals in finance do, what types of decisions they make, on what types of interrelationships they must deal with, and what skills and abilities they must have to be successful.

Source of Information

The articles in Section I have previously appeared in the *Financial Management Collection*, *Financial Management Forum*, and various trade publications. The job descriptions in Section II were compiled from questionnaires which were completed by individuals holding junior, middle, and senior management positions in a variety of corporations throughout the United States and from formal job descriptions provided by the personnel departments of various corporations. Section III consists of articles describing various aspects of education. The material on professional certifications in Section IV was compiled from information provided by certifiaction-sponsoring organizations and a variety of public sources.

TABLE OF CONTENTS

SECTION II-JOB DESCRIPTIONS

ACCOUNTING

BANKING AND FINANCIAL INSTITUTIONS

CONSULTANT-MANAGEMENT LEVEL

CORPORATE FINANCE

CORPORATE TAXES

INSURANCE

INVESTMENTS

REAL ESTATE

WORKING CAPITAL MANAGEMENT

SECTION III-PERSPECTIVES ON EDUCATION

SECTION IV-CERTIFICATIONS AND DESIGNATIONS

WHY FMA IS IMPORTANT TO THE CAREERS OF PRACTITIONERS
J.T. COOK, III

J.T. Cook was the President of the Texas A&M Student Chapter of the Financial Management Association International in 1989 and is currently an account executive at FINOVA capital Corporation in Dallas, Texas. In the years following his graduation, he has become an increasingly active professional member of the Association through positions as a Director-At-Large on the FMA Student Chapters' Committee, FMA Long-Range Planning Committee, and participation at the FMA Annual Meetings.

One of the most important steps a new business graduate can take is to maintain his/her membership in the FMA. All too often in the excitement of getting ready to graduate and preparing for a new job, there is a tendency to let your affiliations lapse with organizations, societies, and clubs that you maintained during your academic career. In one way or another, those organizations, such as the FMA, have served a very supportive role in preparing you to graduate and in finding that perfect first job. It's important to remember that the FMA does not quit working for you once you leave school and that maintaining your membership will prove truly valuable as you take on the new role of "professional." As you begin working in the professional finance sector, it becomes increasingly important to maintain and build on your professional and academic credentials. There are three primary reasons for continuing your professional affiliation with the FMA . These reasons apply to all financial areas, whether your career begins in consulting, banking, investment banking, corporate finance, or continues in academia.

The first reason is an academic one. The FMA serves as a highly respected professional society in academia. Emerging theories in finance and applied concepts are continuously being explored and researched in the academic world. The very latest in research, whether it involves the analysis of stock price movements and returns or the evaluation of investment strategies related to investment banking, is persistently being published by the academic community. Remaining cognizant of changing financial theories, new financial products, and improved financial methods is invaluable to your career path. It may not seem relevant right after you graduate, but chances are that in the future new financial research and innovations will impact you professionally. In the field of litigation support consulting, many areas that are researched in theory are actually put into practice. For instance, in securities fraud claims, the analysis of stock price movements associated with fraudulent or misleading disclosures is sometimes evaluated utilizing an event study approach—an approach which assumes that the true value and price of a security move together except on days where fraudulent information is released. In attending the FMA annual meetings, I've often met the academicians who research the very issues and theories that we put into practice. As you will discover, the FMA assists you in maintaining your learning power and keeps you ahead of the "game". That "game" is keeping yourself aware of the cutting edge of research being developed in the finance world.

The second reason for maintaining your FMA membership is to further your professional development. As you move ahead in your career, maintaining your professional affiliation with other finance practitioners who have similar backgrounds and careers will become increasingly important. The FMA is a good way to network with others who practice the same or similar type of work while building on your own credentials. In addition, the Association provides a number of publications to finance professionals that share information from within the industry and keep you apprised of current events.

The third reason for maintaining your affiliation with the FMA is that the FMA is the premier organization for bridging the gap between the academic and professional finance worlds. In order for the field of finance to progress, it is important that the academic and practitioner worlds work hand in hand. The FMA serves as a catalyst to bring these two worlds together to ensure that what is being researched is also what is being practiced and vice versa. The ability of FMA to facilitate the interaction between the academicians who research issues and theories and the practitioners who put them into practice is evidenced by the success of the FMA Annual Meeting. Through the Annual Meeting, its publications and services, the FMA merges the academic and professional finance worlds and educates its members regarding research in current theory and applications.

In summary, active membership in the FMA as a professional will keep you up to date on emerging financial theories and research applicable to your area of finance. By assisting in the construction and maintenance of a network of professionals in your field and in other fields in finance, the FMA serves as a valuable tool to enhance your professional development. Maintaining your affiliation and membership in the FMA will serve you both individually and credential in optimizing the development of your professional career.

CORPORATE FINANCE

Career Opportunities in Treasury Management

Aaron L. Phillips, University of Akron,
Formerly Managing Director, Research and Information Services
for the Treasury Management Association.
Copyright © 1999, Financial Management Association International.

Financially speaking, what do publicly held corporations, privately held businesses, non-profit organizations, state and municipal governments, and colleges/universities all have in common? The answer may be a surprise. It isn't capital budgeting because most service organizations do not make significant investments in capital projects. It isn't shareholder wealth maximization because governments and other not-for-profit organizations do not have shareholders. It isn't dividend policy because the majority of businesses (as well as the not-for-profits) are not publicly held. And it isn't capital structure.

The one unifying consideration all organizations share, whether publicly held, privately held, government, or not-for-profit, is the concern over liquidity management. It is a safe assumption that a for-profit entity will not remain in business long if it either lacks liquidity or does not effectively manage its liquidity. Empirical research has documented that corporate financial liquidity measures are important for assessing and/or pricing credit, determining bond ratings, forecasting bankruptcy, etc. Similarly, a not-for-profit organization cannot continue to meet its mission objectives, or at the very least risks jeopardizing its relationship with its stakeholders, if it lacks prudent liquidity management. In short, liquidity management is a major concern for every organization. The profession which practices liquidity management as part of its job responsibilities is treasury management.

The purpose of this article is to provide an overview of treasury management. This article draws on several recent research studies conducted by the Treasury Management Association (TMA).[1]

I. PRACTICE OF TREASURY MANAGEMENT

Treasury management historically was centered on working capital management. When double-digit interest rates were common in the late 1970s and early 1980s, effective cash management was critical to an organization's financial well-being. Idle cash carried with it a significant opportunity cost, either in lost investment

---

[1]The Treasury Management Association (TMA) is the world's largest individual membership association devoted to representing individuals engaged in treasury-related activities; its membership is currently in excess of 12,000 members. IMA draws its members primarily from Corporate America, both publicly and privately held firms, but TMA also has a significant number of members employed in non-profit organizations, governmental limits (state and local), as well as at universities and in foreign countries. TMA regularly conducts survey research, either solely or in cooperation with other organizations, to provide information to the treasury profession.

revenue or excess interest payments on lines of credit. The aftermath of the double-digit prime interest rate era finds treasury managing global financing responsibilities and greater levels of financial risk. Today's treasury department, partly a result of corporate re-engineering and partly a result of dynamic changes in the way organizations use technology and information, is more centralized. As a consequence of these changes, the practice of treasury management is becoming broader in its scope of responsibilities and more strategically focused within the organizational structure.

In the spring of 1996, TMA conducted a Job Analysis Survey of the treasury profession to profile the jobs treasury professionals perform. The purpose of this survey was twofold: 1) to determine how important individual job responsibilities are to specific positions, and 2) to determine the knowledge and skills needed by the respondents in those positions to perform their job responsibilities.

Survey respondents were asked to rate each of the 131 job responsibilities and each of the 152 job knowledge/skill items for its importance to their individual position. The scale used in this survey was:

1 = Insignificant	4 = High importance
2 = Low importance	5 = Very high importance
3 = Moderate importance	

Since respondents rated each item for its importance to their specific positions, overall average scores for the items in the survey can be misleading. Individuals who do not have job responsibilities in any particular functional area were observed to rate each of the individual job responsibilities in that area, and most of the related knowledge/skill items, as insignificant. It was necessary, therefore, to distinguish between those individuals having job responsibilities in each functional area and those who do not.

Each of the 10 areas was examined separately. Respondents were considered to have job responsibility in an area if they rated at least one individual responsibility at a level of 4 or higher. Table 1 provides an overview of the respondents who rated at least one job responsibility in a given functional area as high or very high in importance. As indicated, 100% of the respondents in each job title rated at least one General Treasury Management (GTM) item a 4 or 5. This is not unexpected since GTM was used as a category to contain those individual job responsibilities not easily included in one of the other nine areas. Examples of the items in this category include establishing accounts receivable guidelines, credit guidelines, and collection guidelines. Other items in this category include developing contingency plans, monitoring vendor financial conditions, and reviewing and implementing external regulations.

A. Liquidity Management

Liquidity management, as central to treasury management, is clearly evident in the results contained in Table 1. Three areas most closely identified with liquidity management are domestic cash operations, short-term investment management, and short-term borrowing. Effective liquidity management requires that cash be managed through appropriate cash collection and disbursement methods, with excess cash

Table 1. Job Responsibilities by Function

This table provides a summary of the responses by respondents who rated at least one individual job responsibility in a given functional area as high or very high in importance.

	Total Sample	Chief Financial Officer	Vice President Finance	Treas.	Asst. Treas.	Dir. of Treas. Oper.	Mgr. of Treas. Oper.	Cash Mgr.	Sr. Analyst	Analyst
Gen.Treas. Mgmt	100.0%	32 (100.0%)	32 (100.0%)	132 (100.0%)	192 (100.0%)	118 (100.0%)	193 (100.0%)	243 (100.0%)	66 (100.0%)	51 (100.0%)
Domestic Cash Oper.	95.6	31 (96.9)	27 (84.4)	127 (95.5)	179 (92.3)	113 (95.8)	183 (94.8)	241 (98.0)	63 (95.5)	48 (94.1)
Short-Term Inv. Mgmt	79.7	29 (90.6)	28 (87.5)	113 (85.0)	155 (78.7)	88 (74.6)	153 (79.3)	197 (80.1)	39 (59.1)	42 (82.4)
Short-Term Borrowing	78.8	27 (84.4)	25 (78.1)	114 (85.7)	165 (85.1)	88 (74.6)	153 (79.3)	185 (75.2)	42 (63.6)	35 (68.6)
Managing Fin. Inst.[a]	76.7	28 (87.5)	26 (81.3)	112 (84.2)	161 (83.0)	104 (88.1)	149 (77.2)	169 (68.7)	39 (59.1)	24 (47.1)
Info. & Tech Mgmt	70.6	19 (59.4)	19 (59.4)	93 (69.9)	141 (72.7)	93 (78.8)	141 (73.1)	169 (68.7)	43 (65.2)	30 (58.8)
Corp. Fin & Capital Markets	58.7	30 (93.8)	26 (81.3)	112 (84.2)	140 (72.2)	68 (57.6)	98 (50.8)	100 (40.7)	27 (40.9)	21 (41.2)
Int'l Treas. Mgmt	45.4	4 (12.5)	9 (28.1)	67 (50.4)	100 (51.5)	50 (42.4)	89 (46.1)	112 (45.5)	32 (48.5)	18 (35.3)
Employee Funds Mgmt[b]	35.3	24 (75.0)	15 (46.9)	73 (54.9)	80 (41.2)	41 (34.7)	62 (32.1)	49 (19.9)	13 (19.7)	17 (33.3)
Insurance Risk Mgmt	18.8	21 (65.6)	9 (28.1)	60 (45.1)	43 (22.2)	22 (18.4)	27 (14.0)	12 (4.9)	3 (4.5)	2 (3.9)

[a]This category represents managing financial institutions as well as managing investor relationships.
[b]This category includes employee benefits, pensions, and other funds management.

being invested until needed and anticipated shortages being financed with borrowing. The results in Table 1 confirm the importance of this assertion.

Since banks cannot legally pay corporations interest on their checking account balances due to Regulation Q, no business wants to keep idle cash on hand. Therefore, one of the controller's principal activities includes identifying the number and dollar amount of checks clearing a firm's bank accounts each day, moving funds around to cover clearing checks, and liquidating short-term investments as needed.

In addition to managing liquidity, treasury managers can expect to be actively involved in maintaining good corporate-bank relationships. Banks provide many treasury management services, such as checking services, lockbox services, lines of credit, wire transfers, balance reporting, controlled disbursement, etc. To provide high levels of service to your business, banks need to know the business. The business provides information to their banks on changes in the firm's credit needs, check processing volumes, and many other banking services. Controllers/Treasury departments also need to know what services banks can provide and how much they are charging for those services. Consequently, a frequently performed function is reviewing the account analysis statements provided by banks, which detail volume and fees associated with each bank service, and evaluating the relationships with the banks. Those who practice treasury management forecast that financial institution relationship management will become even more important in the future.

Liquidity management occurs in organizations of all sizes and types, including corporations, non-profit organizations, governments, and even colleges/universities. Smaller firms may not have a separate treasury department, but they manage cash never-the-less. Often, this may be performed by accountants whose entry positions include managing accounts receivable and accounts payable. In larger organizations, liquidity management will be found in a formal treasury department, which may have a staff of two to 200.

The majority of respondents in all nine treasury-related positions rate individual job responsibilities associated with liquidity management high or very high in importance. Overall, 95.6% of all survey respondents rated one or more aspects of domestic cash operations as high or very high in importance to their job. Furthermore, nearly 80% of respondents rated one or more aspects of short-term investment management and one or more short-term borrowing responsibilities as high or very high in importance to their jobs.

Table 2 shows the individual job responsibilities for the five functional areas from which the majority of respondents rated items high in job responsibility importance, excluding general treasury management. These five areas, not coincidentally, are the ones most germane to liquidity management. The average column reflects the scores assigned by only those respondents rating one or more individual job responsibilities a 4 or 5 for importance. The average responses from individuals in three distinct treasury positions are displayed for comparison purposes. The scores under the positions of treasurer, manager of treasury operations (hereafter referred to as manager), and analyst indicate the average score assigned to each job responsibility by all survey respondents holding these position titles.[2]

Only the more highly rated individual job responsibilities are listed in Table 2. For example, of the respondents rating one or more domestic cash operations job responsibilities as high or very high in importance (see Table 1), Table 2 shows that establishing the daily cash position was rated highest with an average 4.34 score. When respondents in one of the three separate positions rated other job responsibilities higher in importance, those items are also included. For example, for short-term investment management, analysts are more concerned with providing short-term investment reports than monitoring compliance with investment guidelines when compared to the average rating. By comparison, treasurers are more concerned

---

[2]These three positions represent senior, mid-, and early career individuals. TMA's Eighth Annual Compensation Survey (1996) indicated that 47% of treasurers have 15 or more years in the profession and another 40% have been in it five to 15 years. By comparison, 20% of manager-level respondents have 15+ years in the profession while 64% have five to 15 years of experience. In contrast, 71% of analysts have fewer than five years in the profession and only 15+ years.

6

Table 2. Highest-Rates Liquidity Management-Related Job Responsibilities

This table reports the job responsibility rating for the five functional areas (denoted by panel headings) from which the majority of respondents rated items high in job responsibility importance. The responses were scored in a five-point scale (1=insignificant, 5=very high).

	Average	Treasurer	Manager of Treas. Oper.	Analyst
Panel A. Domestic Cash Operations				
Establishing Daily Cash Position	4.34	4.31	4.19	4.32
Executing Funds Movement Transactions	4.21	4.16	4.14	4.08
Managing Bank Balances	4.19	4.14	4.07	4.06
Managing Daily Corporate Liquidity	4.11	4.18	4.01	3.64
Designing & Maintaining Cash Management Systems	3.90	3.76	3.86	3.33
Implementing/Setting Up Cash Management Services	3.81	3.58	3.76	3.31
Reporting Cash Operations Activities	3.77	3.76	3.72	3.46
Managing Transactions & Resolving Errors	3.76	3.47	3.75	3.92
Preparing Cash Forecasts	3.68	3.83	3.56	3.63
Panel B. Short-Term Investment Management				
Managing Daily Corporate Liquidity	4.30	3.87	3.81	3.67
Executing Investment Transactions	3.97	3.46	3.58	3.78
Monitoring Compliance with Investment Guidelines	3.76	3.48	3.43	3.12
Establishing Investment Guidelines	3.50	3.57	3.22	2.53
Developing Investment Strategies	3.56	3.55	3.33	2.63
Providing Short-Term Investment Reports	3.50	3.08	3.21	3.48
Panel C. Short-Term Borrowing				
Managing Daily Corporate Liquidity	4.32	3.99	3.68	3.34
Executing Borrowing Transactions	3.91	3.63	3.34	3.02
Borrowing or Repaying Principal	3.91	3.61	3.39	3.12
Monitoring Compliance with Borrowing Guidelines and Loan Covenants	3.65	3.68	3.18	2.68
Reporting Short-Term Borrowing Activities	3.78	3.46	3.32	3.18
Panel D. Managing Financial Institution Relationships				
Negotiating Prices and Operating Agreements for Financial Services	4.10	3.90	3.65	2.63
Maintaining Relationships to Meet Credit and Operating Needs	4.02	3.99	3.56	2.82
Establishing Relationship Strategies with Financial Institutions	4.01	3.95	3.50	2.73
Conducting Periodic Reviews with Service Providers	3.90	3.61	3.57	2.66
Panel E. Information and Technology Management				
Implementing and Maintaining Treasury Systems	3.93	3.40	3.48	3.18
Developing Specifications for Treasury Systems	3.72	3.24	3.40	2.65
Developing Guidelines and Strategies for the Purchase & Use of Treasury Systems	3.71	3.23	3.33	2.65

with establishing investment strategies and developing investment guidelines, vis-à-vis managers and analysts, than executing transactions.

Directly related to liquidity management is managing financial institution relationships. Financial institutions are a major provider group of treasury management services, such as cash concentration and disbursement services and short-term financing. Of all respondents, three-fourths rate one or more aspects of it as high in importance (Table 1). The values in Table 2 indicate that both treasurers and managers assign marginally higher average scores to individual institutional relationship management items than short-term investing and borrowing activities. In contrast, those holding analyst positions rate institutional relationship management items below moderate importance to their specific job. Fewer than half of the analysts (47.1%) rated any item in this category high in importance to their job.

Another area significantly impacting treasury operations is information and technology management. The electronic transfer of information and funds within organizations and with external parties allows treasury departments to better manage information and costs while improving liquidity. Because technology applications can represent a considerable financial investment for the treasury department, and have implications for both employment and training, respondents in treasury operations (directors and managers) rate technology responsibilities higher than do others in treasury departments. Approximately three-fourths of the respondents in treasury operations positions (director and manager) rate one or more technology items high or very high in importance. Table 2 shows that managers rate individual technology-related job responsibilities higher than do treasurers and much higher than analysts.

B. Beyond Liquidity Management—The Treasurer's Job

The averages in Table 2 indicate that treasurers are more engaged at the strategic level than at the transaction level. More than any other position, except chief financial officer, they are responsible for developing short-term strategies, monitoring compliance with guidelines, and negotiating for financial services. The analysis also documents that treasury departments, and treasurers in particular, have responsibilities outside of liquidity management. From Table 1 it is evident that over half the respondents have high or very high job responsibility in corporate finance and capital markets. Responsibility in this area, however, falls principally on those more senior in their careers. Table 3 reveals that treasurers rate this job responsibility slightly above moderate (3.0) in importance, which is consistent with the average of respondents categorized as having a high job responsibility here. Although 84.2% of treasurers report a high corporate finance and/or capital markets responsibility, only 50.8% of managers and 41.2% of analysts rate any aspect high for its importance to their jobs. Consequently, the average ratings in this area for both managers and analysts are much lower than for treasurers.

Half of the respondents in any particular position, or fewer, report having any significant international treasury management responsibilities. If they do, their activities center on information management/systems and foreign exchange rate

Table 3. Highly Rated Job Responsibilities Outside Liquidity Management

This table reports the job responsibility ratings for the functional areas outside of liquidity management. The responses were scored on a five-point scale (1=insignificant, 5=very high).

	Average	Treasurer	Manager of Treas. Oper.	Analyst
Panel A. Corporate Finance and Capital Markets				
Administering Long-Term Financing Arrangements	3.47	3.43	2.65	1.85
Monitoring Compliance with Long-Term Financing Policies	3.43	3.31	2.69	1.92
Analyzing & Using Appropriate Financing Vechicles & Techniques	3.32	3.29	2.49	1.81
Analyzing & Managing Interest Rate Risk	3.23	3.17	2.46	1.92
Developing Long-Term Corporate Financial Strategies	3.20	3.27	2.35	1.76
Establishing/Developing Financing Policies	3.12	3.23	2.28	1.65
Panel B. International Treasury Management				
Designing, Implementing, & Administering Treasury Management Strategies & Systems	3.60	2.54	2.51	1.91
Executing & Monitoring Foreign Exchange Transactions	3.47	2.39	2.52	1.94
Establishing Appropriate Procedures to Monitor & Manage Foreign Exchange Exposure	3.02	2.33	2.14	1.45
Forecasting & Monitoring Foreign Exchange Rates	2.85	2.11	2.07	1.68
Panel C. Employee Benefits, Pension, and Other Funds Management				
Assisting in Developing and/or Recommending Investment Policies, Objectives, and Allocations	3.46	2.93	1.96	1.67
Managing Fund Assets or Acting as Liaison to Outside Managers	3.35	2.87	1.85	1.63
Evaluating and/or Selecting Investment Managers	3.26	2.79	1.72	1.66
Managing Funding Requirements	3.24	2.55	1.92	1.65
Panel D. Insurance Risk Management				
Developing Insurance Risk Management Strategies	4.06	2.80	1.55	1.13
Managing Brokerage Relationships	4.03	2.70	1.56	1.21
Identifying, Evaluating, and/or Selecting Insurance Providers	4.01	2.71	1.56	1.15
Assisting in or Developing/Establishing Insurance Risk Management Guidelines	3.95	2.73	1.54	1.17

forecasts and transactions. Average ratings for importance of job responsibilities in this area, shown in Table 3, are attributable to the low percentages of respondents having international treasury management responsibilities, as noted in Table 1; e.g., only one-third of analysts classify any aspect of international treasury management activities as being high in responsibility for their particular job. Two factors contribute to this result. First, among respondents at for-profit organizations, many businesses operate either domestically only or their foreign operations constitute a minor portion of their total revenues/activities. Consequently, international job responsibilities in the treasury departments of profit-oriented businesses carry a lower level of importance than do many other areas of financial management. Second, treasury management responsibilities are performed by governmental units, colleges/universities, and other not-for-profit organizations, which have no significant international activities. Of the survey respondents, 92 (8.6%) fall into these industry groupings.

Contributing to the breadth of treasury management is the involvement of the treasurer's department in employee benefits management and insurance risk management. It is not unusual to find pension and other employee benefits management responsibilities in human resources departments. Treasury departments, however, have traditionally been responsible for investment management activities for the organization. This responsibility, and accompanying ability, allow treasurers to use their expertise to the benefit of other areas of the organization. Of the treasurer respondents, 54.9% indicate responsibility for making investment policy and investment decisions as they relate to employee benefits.

One final specialty area considered is that of insurance risk management; i.e., the risk to the organization's assets and/or activities from accidents and the use of insurance to provide liquidity in the event of an accidental loss. Although few analysts (3.9%) and managers (14.0%) have any insurance risk management responsibilities, nearly half (45.1%) of the treasurers report important job responsibility in this area. As Table 3 indicates, the treasurer's primary focus in this area is on strategy development and managing relationships with service providers.

In summary, analysts, as representing early career treasury executives, operate predominantly in the areas related to liquidity management, with domestic cash management as their primary focus. Areas of collateral importance include short-term investing and borrowing, with some additional responsibility in information and technology. The more senior position of treasurer, however, is a much broader position. The treasurers responding to this survey rate liquidity management strategy, policy, and guideline-type job responsibilities higher in importance than transactional-related items. In addition, the treasurer is responsible for negotiating financial services for a variety of needs, including liquidity management (investments, borrowing needs, cash collection and disbursement, etc.), capital market needs, pension asset investment and administration, and insurance risk management. It is these latter, non-liquidity management, areas which tend to differentiate the treasurer's job from other positions in treasury.

II. Treasury Management Knowledge and Skills

In addition to assessing the importance of individual job responsibilities, the job analysis measured the importance of specific knowledge and skill items respondents indicated they need to perform their jobs. Table 4 lists the highest rated items for knowledge and skill in the areas of liquidity management.

Treasury departments represent the largest user group of the US payments systems; consequently, it is not surprising that respondents indicated they need information in that area to perform their job responsibilities in cash management. It is also evident that information on available cash concentration and disbursement systems rates high in importance for the same reason. In terms of mathematical skills, respondents indicate a high need for information on cash forecasting methods. The ability to forecast cash flows with a given level of certainty implies more effective investment and borrowing activities, the other two major elements essential to liquidity management.

Table 4. Highest-Rated Liquidity Management Knowledge Items

This table reports the most important skills needed to perform liquidity management. The responses were scored on a five-point scale (1=insignificant, 5=very high).

	Average	Treasurer	Manager of Treas. Oper.	Analyst
Panel A. Domestic Cash Operations				
Objectives of Cash Management	4.49	4.31	4.50	4.38
Cash Concentration Systems, Products & Services	4.07	4.02	4.09	3.88
US Payment Systems	4.07	3.95	4.10	3.94
Cash Forecasting Objectives	4.00	4.09	3.92	3.92
Cash Forecasting Methods	3.94	4.02	3.85	3.82
Disbursement Systems, Products & Services	4.05	4.01	4.04	4.06
Collection Systems, Products & Services	4.00	3.91	4.03	4.02
Panel B. Short-Term Investment Management				
Corporate Objectives & Strategies Including Policies & Procedures	4.23	4.13	3.91	3.84
Instruments Available	4.12	3.93	3.84	3.86
Risks Associated with Each Investment	4.05	3.87	3.81	3.53
Timing of Maturities	4.04	3.83	3.77	3.63
Panel C. Short-Term Borrowing				
Corporate Objectives & Strategies Including Policies & Procedures	4.14	4.11	3.73	3.49
Available Sources of Funds	4.10	3.90	3.71	3.63
Timing of Maturities	3.98	3.86	3.62	3.47
Financial Analysis Skills	3.84	3.89	3.56	3.35
Panel D. Managing Financial Institution Relationships				
Product & Operating Capabilities of Financial Institutions	3.82	3.63	3.73	3.18
Service Quality of Financial Institutions	3.81	3.68	3.72	3.30
Pricing & Compensation of Financial Institutions	3.78	3.62	3.63	3.16
Financial Strength of Financial Institutions	3.65	3.76	3.43	3.08
Panel E. Information and Technology Management				
Definitions, Basic Applications & Relationship of EFT, EDI, & Electronic Commerce	4.03	3.76	3.85	3.58
Reasons for Using & Benefits Associated with Electronic Commerce	3.99	3.68	3.78	3.52
Types of Transactions that can be Initiated Electronically	3.87	3.42	3.73	3.64
Uses & Capabilities of a Treasury Workstation	3.85	3.56	3.71	3.38
Services Offered by Major Financial/Information Clearinghouses	3.82	3.52	3.63	3.48

11

Central to treasury management is a thorough understanding of the organization's objectives, including related policies and procedures. Knowledge of corporate and cash management objectives, accordingly, received the highest average scores in the areas of cash operations, short-term investments, and short-term borrowing. Following knowledge of the organization's objectives, respondents indicated that they need to be current in the available sources of funds (in the case of borrowing) and investment choices. Among the different knowledge/skill items, timing of maturities received some of the highest average scores in this area, which is consistent with effective cash management and supports the preparation of cash flow forecasts, documented earlier, as an important job responsibility.

In terms of financial institution relationship management, respondents indicated they need knowledge of financial service product offerings, the quality of those services, and the pricing and compensation for service providers. All three respondent positions included in Table 4 listed these items among the highest rated for the category. Note that the treasurer, as principal risk manager of many organizations, is more concerned about the financial strength of the financial services providers than the other three aspects of financial institution relationships listed.

The job knowledge items for information and technology management receiving the highest average scores in this category, from among the 21 job knowledge/skill items listed in the survey, indicate the importance of technology to treasury management. The extent to which technology application is either changing or being enhanced at a rapid pace is illustrated by the types of skills and knowledge needed in this area. Respondents are in need of information on services available and what they can be used for. Those informational needs include the practical aspects of electronic commerce, such as basic terminology, the benefits of electronic commerce, and the types of transactions which can be initiated electronically. The extent to which treasury workstations, which integrate information (financial and otherwise) across departments, are being perceived as the future of technology application in treasury is illustrated by the rating this item received across treasury positions.

In 1995, TMA conducted a detailed study of the informational needs of the treasury profession. The entire membership of the TMA and a random sample of non-member treasury executives were surveyed to assess, among other things, the areas where they had the greatest need for information. The survey listed 47 areas and asked respondents to rate each item on a seven-point scale, from 1 = very low to 7 = very high, for their individual information need. Table 5 lists those items and the average scores each received.

The results reported in Table 5 confirm the results of the Job Analysis Survey in terms of treasury department information needs and, by implication, treasury department responsibilities. The 15 highest-ranking items are identified with their ranks in Table 5. Among the 15 highest-ranked items in the table, the four under working capital management include items previously noted as central to treasury department responsibilities; i.e., cash management, short-term investing, and short-term borrowing. As previously noted from the job analysis, financial institution relationship management is very important; that observation is confirmed from the Needs Assessment Survey with it being the fourth-highest-ranked item for

Table 5. Informational Needs

This table provides results from a Treasury Management Association survey of the informational needs of the treasury profession. The areas were ranked on a seven-point scale, with 1=very low and 7=very high informational needs.

Area	Rank	Average Rating	Area	Rank	Average Rating
Corporate Finance			***Treasury***		
Capital Budgeting		3.79	Bank/Financial Institution Relations	(4)	5.77
Capital Markets		4.46	Bankruptcy/Financial Distress		3.34
Capital Structure		4.26	Disaster Recovery		4.43
Dividend Policy/Practice		3.39	EDI/EFT	(9)	5.29
Financial Planning		4.56	Information Systems/MIS	(14)	4.95
Mergers/Acquisitions		3.79	Internal Controls	(10)	5.21
Financial Risk Management			International Finance		3.94
Derivatives Pricing/Valuation		3.87	Investor Relations		3.56
Foreign Exchange		3.97	Leasing		3.52
Interest Rate Risk Management	(15)	4.80	Long Term Debt		4.54
General			Pension Management		3.51
Benchmarking	(13)	4.96	Quality Management		4.12
Cash/Treasury Management Practices	(2)	6.06	Risk Management		4.48
Electronic Commerce	(11)	5.04	Treasury Operations	(3)	5.98
Industry Studies		4.64	***Regulatory/Government Relations***		
Re-engineering		4.56	Accounting Rules/Regulations		4.62
Working Capital Management			Corporate Reporting		4.35
Accounts Receivable Management		4.50	Corporate Taxation		3.74
Accounts Payable Management		4.57	Legislation Affecting Treasury	(7)	5.46
Cash Accounting		4.69	Regulations Affecting Treasury	(6)	5.56
Cash Forecasting	(5)	5.73	***Human Resources***		
Cash Management	(1)	6.09	Communication Skills		4.60
Credit Management		4.15	Employee Benefits		3.84
Inventory Management		3.07	Entrepreneurial Skills		3.56
Short Term Debt Management	(12)	4.99	Negotiating Skills		4.74
Short Term Investments	(8)	5.40	Personnel Management/Supervisory Skills		4.58

information need. Respondents indicated that they also have a relatively high need for information about legislation and regulations affecting treasury.

Technology and electronic commerce are recurrent themes in both TMA's Job Analysis Survey and Needs Assessment Survey. Observe that electronic commerce, information systems, and EDI/EFT (electronic data interchange/electronic funds transfer) are among the top 15 information need areas for Needs Assessment Survey respondents. The Job Analysis Survey results discussed previously reported similar need for knowledge/skill in the technology area.

III. CURRICULAR DEVELOPMENT

The results from the surveys discussed herein suggest opportunities for new curricular content. Although the intent is not to sound critical of what is taught in the undergraduate finance curricula at many colleges and universities, the reader may find it difficult to interpret the information otherwise.

Typical introductory finance courses focus on the large, publicly held corporation as the model for financial management. This course is often, appropriately, titled corporate finance. That course, as the foundation for all subsequent student preparation in finance, provides an overview of financial management. Cooley and Heck (1996) surveyed 205 finance faculty about their coverage of topics in the introductory finance course and, in terms of student preparation for entry level careers in treasury management, the news for employers and students alike is not good.

The core finance course in an undergraduate business curriculum is usually titled 'Financial Management' or 'Corporate Finance.' This course covers the basics of time value of money, risk and return, capital structure, capital budgeting, types of securities, dividend policy, some international finance, and working capital management. Pay particular attention to this last area for one very important reason: it's where a corporate finance career starts!

Entry-level positions in many organizations are in the controller's and treasurer's departments where a principal activity is managing corporate liquidity. This means that the department actively forecast the cash inflows and outflows of the organization, using near-term excess inflows to make short-term investments. When the forecast projects a shortfall in funds (more outflows than inflows), the department borrows on previously negotiated credit facilities.

TMA's research results demonstrate that the entry-level analyst, whether at a Fortune 500 company or in a university's treasurer's office, needs preparation to manage the organization's liquidity; i.e., cash flow, short-term investments, and short-term borrowing. Cooley and Heck report that 98.0% of faculty cover the valuation of stocks and bonds, most of them in great detail while only 83.0% cover liquidity (16.5% in great detail) and a modest 63.5% cover cash budgeting (30.0% in great detail). In terms of major topic areas ranked, from 1 = least important to 5 = most important, a surprising 34 respondents (17.1%) ranked cash management as least important while another 81 (40.7%) ranked it just above least important (rank of 2). The subject of short-term financing was ranked least important by 30 respondents (15.0%) and received a rank of second from the bottom by another 57 respondents (28.5%).

The implication for this disparity between what entry-level analysts do and need to know how to do versus what undergraduate finance programs teach translates into an opportunity to develop new undergraduate courses focused on liquidity management.

To carry out these identified job responsibilities, an entry-level analysts' skill set will need to include cash flow forecasting techniques. Knowledge of the term structure of interest rates, the types of short-term investments available (e.g., bankers' acceptances, certificates of deposit, U.S. Treasury bills, etc.) and portfolio management techniques is also required.

While graduate level courses in the subject would certainly be beneficial, evidence TMA regularly collects through its Annual Compensation Survey indicates that

50% of treasurers have an MBA or other master's degree, but only 25% of analysts possess a graduate degree. The content of those new courses should focus on technology applications and mathematical techniques associated with cash forecasting and financial analysis.

IV. CONCLUSIONS

Treasury management, as a profession, transcends the boundary of for-profit publicly held corporations. Every firm needs positive cash flow to stay in business, but they do not all do capital budgeting. Every firm needs managers to project cash flows for purposes of making short-term investment and borrowing decisions, but all firms do not declare dividends. Every government, non-profit organization, and university needs professionals prepared to forecast and manage the organization's cash flow, but they do not have shareholders who are concerned about shareholder wealth maximization. Because of this importance, liquidity management is observed to be the most important financial management job responsibility reported by professionals in treasury departments.

Research conducted by the TMA indicates that entry-level job responsibilities in treasury management focus on liquidity management; specifically, they perform responsibilities in cash management, short-term investing, and short-term borrowing. As a consequence of the apparent light coverage of these topics in the typical college corporate finance course, opportunities exist for faculty to develop courses which provide better career preparation for their undergraduate students who might seek careers in treasury departments at both for-profit organizations and otherwise.

TMA has documented that the role of the treasurer is a broad, strategic one in the organizational structure. The treasurer is responsible for overseeing liquidity management, but he or she also provides risk management, employee benefits management, and financial institution relationship management services to the organization. Acting as an internal consultant, the treasurer provides financial advice to other operating units and manages the daily financing activities of the organization.

Treasury management offers good-paying jobs for those who are not headed to Wall Street, into banking, or a career in insurance or real estate. Treasury managers won't be asked to determine the firm's optimal capital structure nor evaluate changes in its dividend policy. Negotiating mergers and evaluating the pros and cons of issuing more stock or long-term bonds are also decisions managers will not be asked to make. They will, however, be performing a vital service in liquidity management, since the one thing crucial to keeping a firm alive is to manage its liquidity. Businesses are acquired because of strong cash flow, and firms fail because they lack cash flow, making the job an important one in every firm.

This article was adapted from Financial Management, Vol. 26, No. 3, Autumn 1997, pages 69-81

CAREERS IN CORPORATE FINANCE

Samuel C. Weaver, Lehigh University
Formerly Vice President of Hershey Chocolate N.A.
Copyright © 1999, Financial Management Association International.
All rights reserved.

Corporate Finance provides many career opportunities. To better understand the available opportunities, it is important to understand a typical Fortune 200 organization chart. (See Table 1.)

At the top of any Corporation is the Board of Directors with the Chairman of the Board (who usually is also the Chief Executive Officer). Corporate Vice Presidents (or Senior or Executive Vice Presidents) report to the CEO. These Vice Presidents include the VP of Human Resources, VP of Corporate Communications, VP and General Counsel, VP and Secretary, VP of Information Technology, VP of Corporate Development, and the VP of Finance and Chief Financial Officer (one person-two titles). In addition, the President and Chief Operating Officer (one person-two titles) reports to the CEO.

The Vice President of Finance and Chief Financial Officer is the "top" finance person within an organization. Reporting directly to the CFO are the Treasurer, Tax Department, and Controller.

The President and COO has operational responsibilities for each of the operating business units, divisions, subsidiaries, etc. In a typical Fortune 200 company, the President and COO will have responsibilities for numerous business units. Each of those business units will be headed by a President with a staff that includes vice presidents of Sales, Marketing, Procurement, Production, Distribution, and Finance. The business unit's Vice President, Finance reports directly to the Operating Unit's President with a dotted line (representing indirect responsibility) to the CFO.

Although this organization chart is typical, different departmental reporting structures are found. In a smaller organization or even a large, one-division firm, the CFO may hold the additional responsibilities the divisional Vice President of Finance performs.

The highlighted boxes on the organization chart provide appropriate career opportunities for the Corporate Finance professional.

Specific Areas and Entry Level Positions

As previously mentioned, the CFO usually has responsibilities for at least three different areas. The Treasurer is responsible for the financing activities of the Corporation while the Controller is responsible for the financial information about the organization. The tax department is responsible for preparing various tax reports.

Under the Treasurer's Office, various areas and entry level positions exist. Although some of these positions are labeled manager, that is more of a title rather than actual managerial responsibilities for people:

Figure 1. Corporate Finance Organization Chart

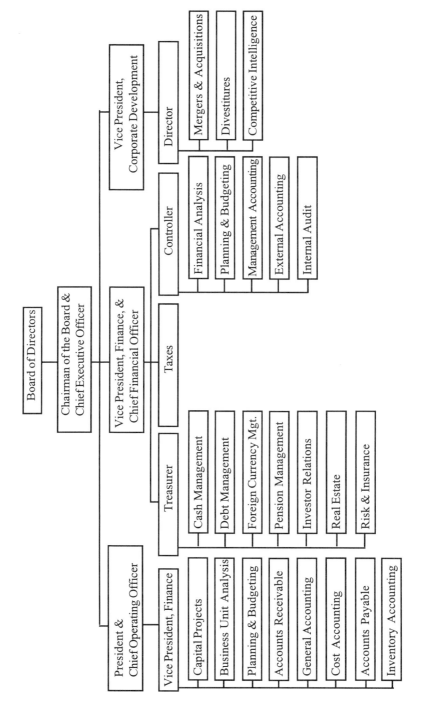

Cash Manager: The cash manager is responsible for day-to-day management of the company's cash balances, marketable securities, and short-term borrowing. Working with operations, the cash manager prepares a detailed cash flow projection that anticipates daily cash receipts and disbursements. Based on these projections, the cash manager anticipates short-term borrowing needs or short-term available cash that can be invested. The cash manager, also, is involved with bank relations.

Debt Manager: The debt manager is responsible for managing the firms intermediate and long-term debt positions. Working with Financial Planning, a detailed financing plan is developed. The debt manager applies the financing plan with a view on anticipated interest rates. When major needs for long-term debt arise, such as acquisitions, share repurchases, the building of a new plant, etc., the debt manager needs to arrange the most flexible financing at the most attractive terms. The debt manager may also have responsibilities for actually repurchasing the Corporation's stock as well as managing the foreign currency exposure.

Foreign Currency Manager: The foreign currency manager is responsible for managing the firm's foreign currency exposure. Working with operations, the foreign currency manager reduces the risk related to foreign operations as well as provides hedges for major transactions such as equipment purchases in foreign currency. The foreign currency manager also works with the derivative markets for foreign currency, forwards and options. The derivative expertise of the foreign currency manager may also be applied to the interest rate derivative markets. In this case, the foreign currency manager may assist the debt manager.

Pension Manager: The pension manager is responsible for managing the firm's pension funds. The pension manager may actually be managing (or co-managing) a small internal pension portfolio with strict guidance to the types of appropriate investments and/or the pension manager may be responsible for day-to-day relationships with external pension fund managers that are employed by the Corporation. The pension manager is, also, responsible for monitoring the quarterly performance of external managers and recommending the addition or deletion of external fund managers.

Investor Relations Analyst: The investor relations analyst is the day-to-day contact person for any stockholder, investment analyst, and general investment community. This position works closely with all areas of the business to better understand the current business position and direction. This position maintains stockholder ownership records, oversees dividend payments, monitors investment analysts' reports for the Corporation as well as the industry, provides specific data as requested by external parties (including fulfilling the request for annual reports), and supports the Director, Investor Relations or CFO in speech writing that is directed towards stockholders. This position is also a public relations position aimed at the corporation's stockholders.

Real Estate Analyst/Manager: The real estate analyst or manager is responsible for managing the Corporation's real estate holdings. This is important in Corporations that are retail oriented such as restaurants, gas stations, convenience stores, retail stores, etc. This position may be responsible for evaluating potential sites for acquisition and making appropriate recommendations.

Risk and Insurance Analyst: The risk and insurance analyst is responsible for securing the broadest insurance coverage at the least expense. Working with all areas of operations and external insurance companies, the risk and insurance analyst identifies potential hazards and seeks to eliminate them. The risk and insurance ` analyst must also evaluate any self-insurance program undertaken by the Corporation.

These positions are typically found within the Treasurer's office.

Under the Controller's office, various areas and entry-level positions exist. Although these positions are not as many in number as in the Treasurer's area, the breadth of the positions is considerably wider.

Financial Analyst: The financial analyst is responsible for a number of areas. In general, the financial analyst is responsible for capital investment valuation, financing analyses, business performance and assessment, and various other finance-related analyses. Capital investment valuation includes setting corporate policy, reviewing capital requests, performing valuations on major capital investments such as acquisitions, self valuations for share repurchase programs, new plants, new products, or business unit valuations. Financing analyses could include evaluating financing alternatives, calculating the cost of capital, determining debt capacity, developing dividend recommendations, evaluating stock split proposals, and recommending lease/buy methodology. More specifically, some of the financing analyses may be completed under the Treasurer's area. However, this is dependent upon the specific organizational design as well as the specific skills available. Business performance and assessment may include analyzing current corporate business conditions, financial benchmarking and industry group analysis, recommending appropriate performance metrics, and providing industry surveys. Various other finance-related analyses could involve compensation studies, measuring corporate productivity, representing finance on various cross-functional projects, etc. The role of the financial analyst can be a wide and varied role or it can be tightly defined within one of the areas noted above.

Planning and Budgeting Analyst: The planning and budgeting analyst is responsible for preparing financial plans (usually at summary levels for a multi-year period) and financial budgets (usually at a very detailed, monthly basis for a fiscal year) in support of the Corporation's strategic objectives. Working with all other areas within the Corporation, the corporate-level planning and budgeting analyst consolidates business plans and budgets. The plans and budgets are presented to Senior Management. It may also be the responsibility of the planning and budget analyst to support Senior Management in establishing reasonable financial goals and objectives for the firm.

As illustrated on the organization chart, other areas may also be reasonable outlets for a career in finance (or related area). Within each of the operating business units, various career opportunities may exist with more of a business operations orientation.

The positions include:

Capital Projects Analyst: The capital projects analyst is responsible for preparing capital expenditure requests. The capital projects analyst works with the various business operations areas. The analyst works with manufacturing and engineering to prepare capital expenditure requests for new equipment, equipment modernization, and new plants. The capital projects analyst, also, works with marketing to evaluate the financial viability of potential new products. From time to time, the analyst may be called upon to present the financial justification as part of the project's approval process.

Business Unit Analyst: The business unit analyst is responsible for business performance and assessment which includes analyzing current business unit business conditions and may include financial benchmarking within a more focused industry group.

Planning and Budgeting Analyst: The planning and budgeting analyst is responsible for preparing financial plans (usually at summary levels for a multi-year period) and financial budgets (usually at a very detailed, monthly basis for a fiscal year) in support of the business unit's strategic objectives. The business unit planning and budgeting analyst prepares the "bottom's up" plan/budget that is consolidated at the Corporate level. The business unit planning and budgeting analyst is, also, responsible for helping the business unit to work towards achieving any "tasking" demanded by Corporate.

Accounts Receivable (or Credit) Analyst: The credit analyst is responsible for determining the creditworthiness of potential customers that want to "borrow" money from the Corporation via accounts receivable. Working within the guidelines of the firm's credit policy, the credit analyst must analyze and evaluate credit applications as well as monitor account collections.

One of the related albeit non-financial areas is within the Corporate Development office of a corporation. Corporate Development includes three areas where a background in finance can be utilized:

Merger and Acquisition Analyst: The merger and acquisition analyst is responsible for evaluating the full breadth of a potential acquisition candidate and may or may not prepare valuations of candidates (see financial analyst, above). Once a candidate has been identified, an appropriate level of management must authorize the acquisition. After management's approval, the merger and acquisition analyst must perform some level of support related to due diligence, deal structuring, and negotiations. When the deal is successfully consummated, the analyst may have some limited operational responsibilities.

Divestiture Analyst: The divestiture analyst is responsible for preparing offering documents for businesses that the Corporation wants to divest. The divestiture analyst needs to work closely with operational management to prepare the required document. The assignment may require close work with an investment banker on specific assignments. This position may also be combined with the merger and acquisition analyst position.

Competitive Intelligence Analyst: The competitive intelligence analyst provides more depth in evaluating and benchmarking competitors and the industry. The competitive intelligence analyst works with all aspects of the business to gather intelligence about competitors' strategy and implementation of that strategy. This intelligence can be gained through research that includes numerous trade associations' publications and meetings. The competitive intelligence analyst is then responsible for providing timely updates to corporate and divisional senior management.

In some organizations, most of the above positions are generalized and broadly called Financial Analysts, although as you can see the focus of the work is varied.

EDUCATION FOR AN ENTRY LEVEL POSITION

The base level education for any of these entry-level positions should include a BS in finance with a strong dose of accounting (at least through the intermediate-level of accounting). Augmenting this education should be statistics, data analysis, business information, and even an advanced accounting course.

An MBA is considered a plus for most of these positions. A finance concentration or business strategy concentration (if the candidate possesses a strong undergraduate finance foundation) is a recommended part of the MBA program.

Certifications, also, demonstrate an independent assessment of technical competency. Appropriate certifications include the CFA (Chartered in Financial Analysis), the CFM (Certified in Financial Management), and the CCM (Certified Cash Manager).

SKILLS FOR AN ENTRY LEVEL POSITION

In addition to the formal education requirements, the successful candidate in any of these positions will be proficient with spreadsheet, word processing, and presentation software. The successful candidate will also have strong communication skills, both written and oral, be of high moral character since most of the information is highly confidential, and understand the benefits of teamwork. In addition, the successful analyst must be flexible, co-operative, professional, and always keep the bigger picture in mind.

ADVANCEMENT AFTER THE ENTRY LEVEL POSITION

The following chart presents the typical analyst "career ladders". As you can see, the three major ladders are planning and budget analysts, financial analysts, and business analysts. Within each ladder, there are three levels, an associate level, an analyst, and a senior analyst.

The planning and budgeting analyst career ladder is restricted to that specific analyst, while the business analyst ladder is often used for corporate development personnel or the most senior of financial analyst. Again, the financial analyst ladder encompasses most of the detailed positions noted above including the Treasurer's positions that are typically labeled as manager, i.e., cash manager.

Initial advancement up a career ladder, may come in 2-5 years. Additional movement is provided via lateral transfers through other parts of the organization.

After an initial career as an "analyst," a manager's role of that technical area could be the next logical step in an individual's career. After a successful manager's

Figure 2. Analyst Career Ladders

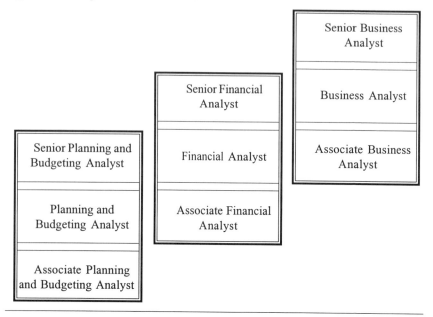

appointment wherein the individual can develop people management skills and a broader business acumen and perspective, the next career step is at a director level. The director has responsibilities for multiple areas, such as the Director, Planning and Analysis. The Treasurer, Controller, and business unit Vice President of Finance are the next career steps within the finance organization followed by the Vice President of Finance and Chief Financial Officer's position.

In addition, other general management (i.e., non-finance) opportunities may be presented to the corporate finance professional. Corporate finance provides a transferable skill set, mindset, and discipline that is valued throughout a Corporation.

Financial Analyst

A DAY IN THE LIFE (CAREER PROFILE)

Financial analysts gather information, assemble spreadsheets, write reports, and review all non-legal pertinent information about prospective deals. They examine the feasibility of a deal and prepare a plan of action based on financial analysis. Being an analyst requires a vigilant awareness of financial trends. Analysts have a heavy reading load, keeping abreast of news stories, market movements, and industry profiles in financial newspapers, magazines, and books. Most analyst jobs are in banking houses or for financial-advising firms, which means following corporate culture and wearing corporate dress. If a deal demands it, they must be prepared to travel anywhere for indeterminate lengths of time. Those who wish to rise in the industry should note the necessity of significant "face time," attending social events and conferences and spending down time with people in the profession, which can be expensive; this social circle tends to gravitate to high-priced attire and costly hobbies, habits, and diversions. Analysts sacrifice a lot of control over their personal lives during their first few years, but few other entry-level positions provide the possibility of such a large payoff come year's end. Many employers use bonuses, which can be equal to or double the beginning analyst's salary, to attract and hold intelligent personnel. Successful financial analysts become senior financial analysts or associates after three to four years of hard work at some firm. Those with strong client contacts and immaculate reputations start their own financial consulting firms. Many work as analysts for about three years and then return to school or move on to other positions in banking. Financial analysts work long hours, and deadlines are strict. "When you have to get the job done, you get the job done. Period," emphasized one. The occasional fifteen-hour day and night spent sleeping in the office is mitigated by the high degree of responsibility these analysts are given. The long hours breed a close kinship. Over 65 percent called their co-analysts extremely supportive, and many labeled them a "major reason" they were able to put up with the demanding work schedule. Most people become financial analysts because they feel it is the best way to immerse themselves in the world of finance and a great way to earn a lot of money. They're right on both counts, but be aware that the immersion is complete and somewhat exclusive, and although people earn a lot of money, few have the free time to spend it all how they'd like to.

PAYING YOUR DUES (MAJOR EMPLOYERS)

Entry-level positions are highly competitive. A bachelor's degree in any discipline is acceptable, so long as the potential analyst's course of study demonstrates an ability to understand and work with numbers. Those with computer science, physical science, or biological science backgrounds may find the field more welcoming than do liberal arts majors. Business majors don't necessarily have an advantage; each company trains the incoming class of financial analysts before they begin the job.

To become a financial analyst you need to have a strong sense of purpose—it is not a job for those who are uncertain that their future lies in the financial world. Candidates must be able to meet and interact with clients, handle a heavy workload, prioritize and complete work under strict deadlines, work as part of a team, and work with computer spreadsheet and valuation programs. Many find the travel stimulating initially, but "after your third week in Jopbsug, Tennessee at the ball-bearing plant, it gets old."

Associated Careers (Who You'll Work With)

Those who progress along corporate financial-analyst tracks can expect to eventually find different jobs in the financial community, perhaps as investment bankers, investment advisors, or financial consultants. Those who enjoy the more interpersonal side of finance move into management consultant positions, where they can use their people skills as well as their financial skills. Over 45 percent head to business school within five years and another ten percent go to law school. A few become in-house financial advisors or officers in the industries they covered as financial analysts.

Past and Future (Major Associations)

The obligations of today's financial analyst were covered by more experienced individuals as late as the 1970s, but with rapid deregulation of ownership in industries in the early 1980s and the rapid growth of the financial sector during those same years, the need arose for a structured and continuing stream of intensively trained professionals familiar with the financial industry. Larger firms, which consolidated their programs in the early 1990s, are cautiously beginning to expand them again, finding opportunities in such new and developing industries as software development, biotechnology, and aerospace technologies.

Quality of Life

Two Years Out: Long hours, low base pay, and a fair amount of responsibility characterize the early years. Analysts travel, pore through documents, meet with clients (on a highly supervised basis) and prepare valuation analyses. They work together on teams that are rotated quickly when needed. Lack of control over hours and personal life are common in the first two years. The burnout rate is surprisingly low in the beginning—around eight percent—because most who enter the industry have few illusions about the demands the job will place on them.

Five Years Out: At the five-year mark, those who remain have achieved the rank of "associate" or "senior financial analyst." Responsibilities shift from producing to pitching, and client contact increases. Many study for professional degrees during these years. Over 70 percent of those who began in the field have either changed firms, returned to school, or changed jobs within the industry. While loyalty is tangible between analysts, the same sense of fidelity doesn't seem to apply to the companies that employ them. Salaries remain relatively stable but bonuses, which once were merely large, can become astronomical; hours, for those who are successful, can actually increase.

Ten Years Out: Successful financial analysts have moved on to vice-presidential positions in the investment banking, financial analysis, or valuation departments of the company. While bonuses still account for the bulk of income, salaries are significant as well. Hours can decrease but responsibility increases and pressure develops to solicit new business. Responsibilities also include personnel decisions and hiring.

CAREER PROFILE

# of people in profession:	700,000
% male:	75
% female:	25
average hours per week:	55
average starting salary:	$ 22,500
average salary after 5 years:	$ 40,000
average salary after 10 to 15 years:	$190,000

PROFESSIONALS READ:

Money, Wall Street Journal

BOOKS, FILMS AND TV SHOWS FEATURING THE PROFESSION:

Money Up Money Down, The Assessment, Wall Street, Dealmaking

MAJOR EMPLOYERS:

Chicago Stock Exchange, Inc.
440 South LaSalle Street
Suite 514
Chicago, IL 60605
Tel: 312-663-2526
Fax: 312-663-2669

American Stock Exchange
86 Trinity Place
New York, NY 10006
Tel: 212-306-1210
Fax: 212-306-1218
Contact: Allison Katz

YOU'LL ASSOCIATE WITH:

Accountants, Bankers, Investment Bankers, Researchers

MAJOR ASSOCIATIONS:

Association for Investment Management and Research
P.O. Box 3668
Charlottesville , VA 22903
Tel: 804-977-6600
Fax: 804-963-6842
Contact: Human Relations Department

Financial Executives Institute
10 Madison Avenue; P.O. Box 1938
Morristown , NJ 07962
Tel: 973-898-4600
Fax: 973-898-4649
Contact: Barbara Dastgheib

American Financial Services Association
9190 18th Street, N.W.
Washington, D.C. 20006
Tel: 202-296-5544
Fax: 202-223-0321

Investor Relations as a Profession

Recruiter and NIRI Surveys profile IR Job and career
Published by the National Investor Relations Institute.
Copyright © 1999, All rights reserved.

The National Investor Institute (NIRI) was founded in 1969 and is an international organization with more than 4,400 members. Our members include the majority of the largest publicly held corporations in the U.S. and an increasing number of small and mid-sized companies.

Capitalizing on career opportunities for investor relations people dictates possessing strong financial and communications skills combined with the ability to meet the growing challenge of expanded responsibilities.

We need to know our companies, know how to market them, know how to integrate our function with related activities of equal importance to the business, perhaps be able to direct all those functions, and have the personal traits that make us capable of operating at the highest levels of management.

Not only does that undoubtedly sound like the ideal job description to many of us, but it also is a realistic appraisal of the responsibilities and requisites that will define the investor relations position in the future, according to the results of NIRI's 1996 membership survey.

The key finding of the 1996 NIRI study is that the duties of the chief investor relations officer are expanding. The large majority (over 80 percent) consults directly with senior management on how the investment community perceives competitors and in providing general market intelligence. Two out of three (64 percent) regularly provide information to their company's Board of Directors–up from 52 percent in 1994. Forty-percent frequently make presentations to the Board.

The study provides unmistakable evidence that investor relations officers believe that investor relations is growing in importance to the company and senior management. Top management's support for and involvement in investor communications is extensive and reported to be on the rise. IR officers are being asked to provide strategic insight into the investment community and are participating in an increasing array of corporate activities.

The function rather than the "segmented, narrowly focused role" of the past now has increased involvement in such areas as strategic planning and corporate advertising while expanding such traditional activities as financial meetings.

Investor relations has shifted from being defensive in posture to more on the offensive. IRO are more proactive in their IR programs and as a consequence their job is broader and some of the things they are asked to do are outside the confines of IR.

CHALLENGING ISSUES FOR IROs

From a list of eight issues, three singled out as very challenging by a majority of the senior investor relations officers. 1) Coping with the short-term perspective of the investment community (65 percent), 2) Building investment interest of the buy-side (62 percent) and 3) Building interest of the sell-side (53 percent).

The primary responsibilities of IR departments center on investment professionals – including relationships with and presentations for analysts, portfolio managers and brokers (each judged to be the prerogative of the IR function by over 80 percent). About three out of four IR programs (73 percent) also manage shareholder identification and analysis.

The primary corporate planning activities in which IR departments are heavily involved continue to be coordinating the annual shareholders' meeting and crisis communications (67 percent and 58 percent, respectively).

Other activities placed under the leadership of investor relations in more than half of NIRI member companies, include oversight of the content for the IR Web site (81 percent), annual reports (68 percent), presentations to the board of directors on IR activities (64 percent) and financial media relations (61 percent).

To keep the investment community informed, virtually all companies conduct one-on-one meetings (98 percent) and participate in group sessions sponsored by others (92 percent). More than three out of four companies also hold analysts conference calls (79 percent) and initiate their own group meetings with important investors (77 percent).

When asked to indicate the types of meetings expected to become more important to their companies' IR programs over the next few years, IROs most frequently pointed to the one-on-one format (cited by 43 percent). About one in three also believe that self-initiated group meetings (34 percent) and analysts conference calls (31 percent) will play more critical roles in their IR programs in the years to come.

PURSUING INDIVIDUALS

Relationships with and group meetings for individual investors also are reported to be the primary concern of most IR officers (87 percent and 80 percent respectively). Other individual investor programs, such as oversight of the transfer agent and proxy solicitation are reported to fall somewhat less often under IR's purview (47 percent and 37 percent respectively).

Virtually all NIRI corporate member companies (96 percent) will have a web site by the end of 1999. Eighty-six percent currently have a web site compared to 55 percent in 1996. Among companies with Web sites, 86 percent report that a section devoted specifically to IR is included.

In the NIRI survey, investor relations practitioners indicated they felt that 52 percent was the optimal desired level of institutional ownership. Interestingly, actual level as reported by respondents, was 57 percent.

When asked to rate the impact several criteria have on the valuation of their company's equities, IROs identify two as being most critical – earnings growth and the quality of senior management. Two other factors – the company's long-term strategy and industry conditions – also are deemed very important. Dividends are least often seen as being significant.

The survey also sought to develop a profile of the investor relations professional.

Practitioners have an average of 6 years of working investor relation's experience. Years of experience vary by company's market capitalization. The average length of investor relations service among large-cap IROs is slightly lower (five years) than among mid- and small-cap firms (eight and seven years respectively). It can be hypothesized that this reflects the somewhat higher extent to which IR is treated as a rotational position in large-cap companies.

Concerning titles, 42 percent are directors, 25 percent are vice presidents and 19 percent are managers. Less senior titles such as IR coordinator, associate, specialist and representative are held by 7 percent.

COMPENSATION IN $120,000S

Average cash compensation (salary plus bonus) of investor relations officers is $120,500, according to a 1999 study. This figure reflects the compensation information for all investor relations officers spending the majority of their time on IR activities. IR executives in the smallest-cap companies earn an average of $97,500 compared to $110,500 in mid-cap firms and $144,200 in large-caps.

IROs who have backgrounds in finance and strategic planning earn the highest salaries. Specifically, total cash compensation (salary plus bonus) is $134,700 for those who have been involved with strategic planning and $133,500 for those with financial experience.

By way of background, some 49 percent of the respondents have a financial background, 24 percent come from communications or public relations fields, 21 percent from marketing or sales and the remaining have experience in administration, strategic planning, operations, human resources or M&A activities.

The trend has been away from corporate communications in favor of finance. The position reports more often to the CFO or treasurer. However, nearly one in four IR departments (23 percent) reports to the CEO, president or chairman. Small-cap and mid-cap companies are more likely to indicate that IR reports directly to the top executive at the company than in large firms.

Average annual budget for IR programs is $490,000. These figures include salaries but not costs associated with the annual report, stock market fees and allocated overhead.

IR LOOKING AHEAD

Written for and published in NIRI's Investor Relations Quarterly, Volume 2, Number 4 by Smooch S. Reynolds, Principal, The Repovich-Reynolds Group

Investor relations, in many ways, faces a future not unlike that of the traveler in Robert Frost's poem "The Road Not Taken." But instead of just two paths, IR has several paths of nearly unlimited possibilities, in terms of corporate influence and career growth. Historically, the investor relations function has shifted from that of a finance-driven role to a communications-driven one and then back again to a role more heavily weighted in finance. But no matter what the past definition, it has always been singular in its focus – and rarely has it encompassed more than one corporate or functional discipline at a time.

Today, in most companies, the function is emerging into a blend of an entire portfolio of career experiences that go beyond just finance-driven investor relations and/or corporate communications and financial public relations. Never have the markets, both financial and employment, been so ripe for a functional area to expand into a greater sphere of corporate influence, increased credibility with Wall Street and higher career potential as they are today.

The investor relations function of the 1990s encompasses financial, communications and brand marketing disciplines. This triumvirate skill base has become the hallmark of today's investor relations officer, and it has also emerged as one of the most successful profiles for this profession in the eyes of the Wall Street community. Senior management teams increasingly expect their investor relations officers (and departments as well) to use a blend of financial acumen, corporate communications positioning expertise and overall brand marketing techniques as a means of communicating with Wall Street constituencies and corporate stakeholders. In addition, corporate management has finally recognized the importance of communicating the company's investor messages to internal constituencies – an activity that was rarely even considered in the past.

Another trend that has emerged in the marketplace relates to the profiles of professionals' career paths that have led them to the investor relations function. The careers of an increasing number of professionals have moved and are moving in a cross-functional direction before they enter the investor relations profession. Included in those functional moves might be tenure in the finance function; a chapter in a line management/operations role and/or serving as head of an operating group; a handful of years in marketing and sales; and then a move into investor relations. With this breadth of knowledge and hands-on functional experience, the investor relations professional is emerging as one of the most highly valued members of the senior management team.

The value that a cross-functional practitioner brings to corporate management is considerable. That same value is also brought to myriad Wall Street constituencies and corporate stakeholders. Imagine the increased credibility that arises from intimate, hands-on experience and knowledge about a wide variety of functional areas – knowledge of the inner workings of an organization is quite powerful in communicating with the very constituencies that affect the valuation of a company's operations.

There are already hints in the marketplace that the chief investor relations role will be defined even more broadly in the next millennium. Marketplace indicators include:

- An increase in the number of professionals with a broader blend of functional career experience who are entering into the investor relations profession;

- The expectation on the part of corporate boards that the company's investor relations executive has broader knowledge of the overall business and not merely the ability to communicate with Wall Street;

- Shareholder activism, which has meant that the investor relations officer must be more astute than ever about both the internal operating/financial issues and the perceptions of all external constituencies (large and small), whose roles have become more influential in recent years; and

- The increased involvement of the Securities and Exchange Commission in broader corporate behavioral and policy issues, resulting in the expectation that the investor relations function include knowledge of myriad issues facing an organization, across all functions. Additionally, this involvement will also move the investor relations function into a leadership role in terms of managing risk, as it is related to both the tangible and intangible inner workings of an organization.

All of these indicators point to the investor relations professional being asked to serve in a leadership capacity, managing functions beyond the obvious. Included in this portfolio might be corporate development, strategic planning and global brand marketing – and possibly even sales and marketing. With this breadth of purview, the investor relations officer has an opportunity to become one of the most influential individuals inside a corporation. It also provides an opportunity for the IRO to navigate his or her career down a track that logically might evolve to elevation to chief executive, truly validating the importance of investor relations.

FINANCIAL ENGINEERING

Careers in Risk Management and Financial Engineering

Jack S. Rader, CFA
Executive Director of Financial Management Association International.
Copyright © 1999, Financial Management Association International.
All rights reserved.

The use of financial and non-financial derivatives by large numbers of firms in recent years has created an entirely new discipline commonly referred to as financial engineering and/or risk management. The scope of this discipline goes well beyond the insurance activities that have traditionally been captured under the title risk management.

Risk management and financial engineering careers can be pursued with organizations that have risks they wish to manage in some fashion. These organizations might be financial or non-financial firms, or they might be manufacturing or service firms. Additionally, there are numerous career opportunities within banks, other financial institutions and exchanges that develop and provide risk management products to end-users.

WHAT ARE RISK MANAGEMENT AND FINANCIAL ENGINEERING?

Risk management is frequently associated with hedging—the reduction in or elimination of a type of risk (e.g., the price risk of a commodity or the market risk of investing in equities). However there is more to it than that. Risk management also can be used to selectively increase exposures to a type of risk in pursuit of additional returns.

Financial engineering refers to the process of designing contracts or derivative securities that allow increased or decreased exposures to risks of various types. Thus, like risk management, financial engineering requires identifying risks that can be managed. Financial engineering goes a step further, however, and designs solutions to specific risk management problems by developing contracts or instruments that allow users to change their exposure to a given risk factor. Forward contracts, future contracts, swaps, OTC options, and exchange-traded options are the instruments most frequently used to manage risk.

There is an old marketing axiom that says where there is a need, an institution or product will arise to fill that need. This is an apt characterization of the nature of financial engineering. Every year, a number of new products are introduced either by exchanges or by large banks and other financial institutions (the OTC market). If a risk to be hedged or an opportunity to be exploited can be identified, it is virtually certain that someone will construct a product that, at least conceptually, allows exploitation of the opportunity or mitigation of the risk.

For example, consider inverse floaters, indexed notes, leveraged bonds, and index-amortization notes. These structured notes, hybrids of debt and various options, became quite popular in 1993 and 1994 as investors were faced with maturing high-

32

yield securities that had to be replaced with much lower yielding securities. In essence, structured notes offered a variety of ways for investors to increase yield through taking on additional market risk. Similarly, interest rate swaps, equity swaps, and commodity swaps all offer firms opportunities to either convert variable rate/ variable price commitments to fixed rate/fixed price commitments, or vice versa. And products like weather derivatives, shipping derivatives, and catastrophe bonds offer firms new ways to raise capital and investors new ways to invest their funds.

According to a number of surveys compiled by Smithson (1996), non-financial firms use risk management products most often for interest-rate, foreign-exchange, and commodity risk management, as well as financing (obtaining funding) and trading. Additionally, non-financial corporations use risk management techniques to reduce fluctuations in cash flow and accounting earnings and to protect the appearance of the balance sheet. Financial firms use risk management products to reduce and/or increase exposure to such risks as volatility, currency, concentration, prepayment, interest rate, liquidity, equity, credit, and counterparty risk.

TYPES OF JOBS

The demand for people who are knowledgeable about risk management and the financial engineering that makes it possible is related to the increasingly complex global environment in which corporations and other organizations find themselves. Additionally, it is a function of the innovation of financial markets and the speed with which new products come to market. And, of course, the demand for risk management—and for people who know how to do it—is driven by the flexibility, leverage and low cost associated with derivative contracts along with the never-before-available avenues for risk management they offer. In recent years, a number of highly publicized losses have been associated with derivatives. These losses, interestingly enough, did not reduce the demand for risk management products as much as it drove home the importance of having competent people who have the requisite knowledge to understand risk and the uses and variety of derivatives available to manage risk.

The types of jobs that are available in financial engineering include the following:

Trader—executes trades in derivative contracts on exchanges to offset portions of the position exposure faced by the firm that provides financial engineered products

Position Manager—responsible for analyzing the net exposure of the firm's positions and developing strategies to manage that exposure

Product Development Analyst—designs and evaluates products to address existing or anticipated client needs

Research Director—directs teams of quantitative analysts who design new products and/or research areas that appear fertile for further product development

Institutional Sales Representative—calls on current and potential clients to assess risk management requirements and suggest ways to manage risks; interacts with product development and research teams

Risk management positions generally are found in the treasury function or on the finance staff of the firms that use the products developed by financial engineers. Traditionally, risk managers for manufacturing and non-financial service firms have had to be knowledgeable in insurance products and the insurable risks faced by firms. Today, however, the requisite knowledge extends well beyond insurance, because the alternatives available to manage a diverse set of risks has increased. Job titles vary widely depending on the industry and the firm. Similarly, the responsibilities vary, depending primarily on the nature and complexity of the risks faced by the firm.

PREPARING FOR A CAREER IN RISK MANAGEMENT AND FINANCIAL ENGINEERING

Financial engineers must have strong quantitative skills and strong mathematics backgrounds. Additionally, they must be well versed in finance and economics, and should understand the implications of relevant accounting pronouncements. Computer usage is an important part of the job as is the ability to deal with complex situations. Risk managers need similar skills, although the requirements for math and quantitative skills are not as high.

Virtually all finance courses are helpful to those who aspire to careers in risk management and/or financial engineering. Understanding the nature and types of risk is essential. Additionally, it is necessary to understand how risk factors (e.g., interest rates) change over time and under varying market conditions.

Universities frequently offer financial engineering courses; some even offer majors in financial engineering. Students who are interested in risk management should take these same courses and pursue some studies in insurance as well. Ultimately, however, the successful financial engineer will not only be able to design useful products but also will be able to market the products, communicating his/her knowledge of risks and risk management solutions to potential and current clients of the firm. Thus, coursework outside the finance area can be important.

Reference

Smithson, C.W., 1996, Managing Financial Risk: 1996 Yearbook, CIBC Wood Gundy.

Comprehensive Personal Financial Planning: A Career Opportunity Worth Considering

Lawrence J. Gitman, Professor of Finance, San Diego State University.
Peter W. Bacon, Professor of Finance, Wright State University.

INTRODUCTION

Financial Planning is the process of determining whether and how an individual can meet his of her life goals through proper management of financial resources. As a career, financial planning is a relatively new field. It emerged as a concept 20 years ago and has steadily evolved to become a valuable service profession that is needed by many Americans. The increasing demand for the services of financial planners developed in response to a variety of social, economic, and demographic changes including:

- New and sophisticated investment media including options, futures, and other derivatives

- Increasingly complicated tax laws

- Increased life expectancies

- Difficulty in planning for longer retirement periods and long-term health care needs

- A blurring of distinction between financial institutions

- Rapidly rising costs of higher education

These and other changes and trends have stimulated a need for a new breed of financial professional—one who is knowledgeable in all aspects of personal financial decision making including personal budgeting, tax planning, investing, real estate broker, tax advisor, lawyer, or accountant is the integration of all facets of a client's financial affairs into a single comprehensive personal financial plan.

WHAT IS COMPREHENSIVE PERSONAL FINANCE PLANNING (CPFP)?

Comprehensive Personal Financial Planning (CPFP) is a process involving the translation of personal financial objectives into specific plans and finally into financial arrangements which implement those plans. It is important to recognize that CPFP is a process: it is not a single step or a single product. The six steps generally associated with the financial process are as follows.

Step 1: Establish the Client-Planner Relationship. When a professional financial planner is engaged by a client to assist him or her in developing a comprehensive personal financial plan, the client-planner relationship must be clearly defined. The planner must explain and document the services that will be provided to the client. The responsibilities of both planner and client must clearly be defined. Compensation arrangements must be clear and acceptable to the client, and the term of the professional relationship should be clear to both parties. Completion of the step is an important prerequisite to the development and implementation of an affordable comprehensive personal financial plan.

Step 2: Gathering Client Data, Including Goals. In order to plan, certain basic information must be gathered about such things as investments, insurance, employee benefits, tax situations, wills, assets, liabilities, risk tolerance levels, and more. Of equal importance is information on client objectives and goals. While each client's personal objectives differ in terms of his or her individual circumstances, in general, the goals of most people can be generally classified as follows:

- Protection against the personal risks of premature death, disability, property and liability losses, unemployment, and large medical care expenses.

- Capital accumulation for emergency fund purposes: education, retirement, and financial independence.

- Provision for retirement income.

- Reduction of the tax burden.

- Planning for estate distribution.

- Investment and property management

Step 3: Evaluation and Consideration of Alternatives: The third step involves analyzing a person's present financial position relative to his/her objectives and the consideration of alternative ways of remedying any deficiencies.

Step 4: Development of the Plan: The actual plan itself should be comprehensive and cover every aspect of one's financial affairs. A true plan should be written. Normally, the plan will include recommendations in the areas of investments, insurance, taxes, retirement funding requirements, estate planning, and personal budget recommendations.

Step 5: Implementation: One of the too often neglected steps in the planning process is a procedure for implementing the plan. This often includes the actual purchase of financial services and products such as insurance policies, annuity programs, specific securities, etc. The key point is that the plan is useless unless implemented.

Step 6: Review and Revision: The financial plan should be regularly reviewed. As circumstances change, so should the financial plans. Therefore, a procedure should be adapted for periodic review and revision as part of the planning process. It should be clear from a review of the steps in planning that coordination of effort is important in carrying out the CPFP process. Personal financial planning requires expertise from a variety of specialized fields such as taxes, investments, insurance, estates, and trusts, etc. Science many experts are normally needed to prepare a comprehensive personal financial plan, the need for coordination becomes very important. What is needed is an integration of the specialties into a cohesive whole that is approached from the viewpoint of the consumer's overall objectives. Thus, coordinated and comprehensive approach to financial planning is required.

THE BASIC ELEMENTS OF A COMPREHENSIVE PERSONAL FINANCIAL PLAN INCLUDE:

- Cash flow/budgeting analysis
- Insurance needs (life, disability, property, etc)
- Employee benefits
- Investment management
- Analysis of debt
- Portfolio analysis
- Closely held business
- Retirement planning
- Forecasting retirement benefits and costs
- Income tax planning
- Estate planning
- Educational funding requirements

It can be seen that these elements fully address the objects included in Step 2 of the CPFP process described above. Three key requirements of the plan are: (1) it must deal with every aspect of an individual's financial affairs; (2) it must be in writing; and (3) it must be developed by professionals who are qualified in the technical fields involved in the planning process, or it can't be relied upon.

CAREER AND EMPLOYMENT OPPORTUNITIES

Financial planners practice a great variety of occupations. While more than one-third of these individuals operate as sole practitioners, many others use their expertise in a variety of environments including human resource and employee benefits departments, credit unions, charitable giving and university development offices, brokerage firms, insurance agencies, accounting firms, and law offices. Recent college graduates will find that many entry-level jobs are likely to be sales-oriented positions in the financial planning department of a financial services firm. Most accounting firms are now offering financial planning services and will hire recent graduates. There are also entry-level positions in the offices of established financial planning firms.

BECOMING A CPFP PROFESSIONAL

In order to become a CPFP professional, it is recommended that the individual pursue a professional certification program. The dominant and most widely recognized of these programs is the Certified Financial Planner (CFP) program, administered by the Certified Financial Planner Board of Standards (CFP Board). The certification requirements established by the CFP Board include the four E's: education, examination, experience, and ethics.

Education: To become a certified financial planner, a candidate must complete a registered financial planning curriculum. Approximately 90 colleges and universities have registered their programs with the CFP Board, including three institutions offering programs on a self-study basis. Each of these institutions offers a curriculum that addresses all aspects of CPFP and is offered at the upper-division level or higher.

Examination: When a candidate has successfully met the education requirement, he or she is eligible to apply for the certification examination. This exam is a 10-hour examination, divided into one four-hour session (Friday) and two three-hour sessions (Saturday). The exam includes three major case problems and is designed to assess your ability to apply financial planning education to financial planning situations in an integral format.

Experience: The CFP program also requires financial planning-related work experience. The amount of required experience varies with the educational background of the candidate. For example, candidates with an undergraduate degree in financial planning are required to have three years of experience while those without an undergraduate degree must have five years of experience.

Ethics: CFP candidates must agree to uphold the CFP board's Code of Ethics and Professional Responsibility. They must also disclose past or pending business-related litigation or proceedings, and acknowledge the right of the CFP Board to enforce this Code through due process.

CONCLUSION

Financial planning is a valuable service profession that is sorely needed by most people. Changing social, economic, and demographic forces ensure that financial planning will continue to increase in importance. Financial planning professionals find satisfaction and challenge in their work. They closely work with other professionals, they have excellent earning potential, and they make a real contribution to their client's economic well being. CPFP is certainly a career opportunity worth considering.

INVESTMENTS

Career Advice for Entering the Investment Profession (An Interview)

Robert R. Johnson, CFA, Ph.D.
Association for Investment Management and Research,
Vice President, Curriculum & Exams.
Copyright © 1999, Financial Management Association International.
All rights reserved.

We talk to many finance students who are interested in becoming security analysts, and they ask a number of questions. What qualities does a potential employer look for in an entry-level analyst? Do I need an MBA or a CFA charter? What future trends should I be aware of? To help answer these questions, we called Mr. David Yu, CFA, Principal, Perigee Investment Counsel in Toronto; Ms. Lynn Gilliland, CFA, Senior Vice President - Director of Investment Research, Northern Trust Company, Chicago; Mr. Yusaf Samad, CFA, Head of Fund Manager Relations - Europe, Citicorp, London. The following is a composite of these conversations.

Lynn, when you are recruiting entry-level analysts, what qualities and characteristics do you look for?

"I look for a keen interest in the investment business. A standard question I ask applicants is what they read regularly. Those who have more than a superficial interest or want to get into the business for the right reasons should have, at a minimum, a subscription to the Wall Street Journal and/or Investors' Business Daily. I regard highly an interest in related publications and books. I also want a person who is naturally curious, and asks thoughtful questions, someone who is interested in how the investment analysis process works and what it requires. Excellent verbal and communication skills are a must. Finally, personality is a major factor. How a person will fit within our corporate culture is very important to us."

David, would you like to add anything?

"Yes. I would add that the job candidate must exhibit good interpersonal skills. Our business, whether the buy side or the sell side of the Street, is essentially a people business. Analysts must be comfortable with people. To be successful, they must be able to communicate, to listen, and to earn other's trust. We can gain a good idea of how comfortably the job candidate relates to others by finding out how active he or she has been in student groups, community associations, or professional societies."

Yusuf, what courses should the student take in preparation for a career as an analyst?

"Analysts should have a solid grounding in the quantitative techniques taught in a business statistics course, and in accounting, economics, financial analysis, corporate finance and portfolio theory. They should also have spreadsheet skills such as being able to use Excel and Access at an advanced level. In addition, because the field of investments is an international environment, fluency in languages other than English is helpful.

David, do you require an MBA or CFA charter for your entry-level positions? What about more senior positions?

"For an entry-level position, we do not require an MBA or CFA charter. A college degree from an appropriate discipline would be a bare minimum in terms of qualifications. We prefer applicants to have accumulated one to two years of investment or related work experience. If a candidate has taken the initiative to enroll in the CFA Program, that increases his or her chances of passing the first screen we apply to entry-level analysts."

"For a more senior position, a CFA charter is a must. An MBA without a CFA charter is acceptable, but the candidate must be well into the CFA Program. These positions demand six to eight years of related work experience."

Lynn, would you like to add anything?

"We do not require either an MBA or CFA charter, but it is definitely a p us if the candidate has one or both or has begun either process. We certainly expect our senior analysts to have such accreditation (although there are always exceptions)."

Yusuf, does your firm provide financial support for master's programs or the CFA Program?

"Our firm encourages and provides financial support for both master's programs and the CFA Program. Many of our employees have enrolled in evening MBA programs at local colleges and have received support for this education from the firm. For the CFA examinations, our firm bears the costs of the examination, the books, and even review programs."

David, would you like to add anything?

"We encourage our staff to become involved in the CFA Program. It is becoming THE designation for the investment business. Our firm provides financial support for the CFA Program and we give employees time off to prepare for the exam."

Yusuf, what industry trends do you believe students should be aware of?

"Students should keep in mind that we live in a global economy. Despite the recent turmoil in global markets, globalization of business will continue to evolve, and investment management is becoming multiproduct, multichannel, and multilocation. Students should be aware of trends around the world and should understand different cultures and languages and the link among various countries and markets (the level of connections are many). Globalization of investment management has significant implications for careers: Investment analysts and managers must be prepared to live in different places around the world, perform different functions during their careers, and understand different types of products and customers."

"Another trend is the importance of scale in our business, which is experiencing increasing competition and higher costs because of demands from the customers. Achieving scale for an investment firm is a challenge. For example, maintaining investment performance at a high level is more difficult as size increases. Many firms are specializing and pursuing well-defined proprietary processes. A student's career expectations have to, therefore, take this into account."

"Finally, risk management is receiving greater emphasis in investment management firms. Managing money in the future will incorporate risk considerations more explicitly than in the past. Resources are being deployed to develop better definitions of risk and to build tools that can deal with the new derivative instruments."

David, would you like to add anything?

"Our industry is changing so fast that keeping up with what is required for success is becoming more and more challenging. It is getting more quantitative and more computer intensive. Investors are more educated and demand more than basic information. If they can't get what they want from one firm, there are 99 other investment firms who will be happy to provide what they want. Therefore students need to always stay up to speed on the latest news, latest tools, and latest research so that they can provide clients with sound, logical solutions to their financial needs."

Lynn, what advice would you give students who want to get into the investment business?

"First, begin to attain the proper credentials. Second, immerse yourself in the information available-read, invest your own funds. Third, network with others already in the business to gain understanding of how things work. Finally, if you can't find the ideal investment job, find something in the industry that is as closely related as possible. Don't settle for something outside the industry in hope of breaking into it later."

Yusuf, would you like to add anything?

"Investment management is a growth business because of the underlying demographics driving the need for long-term savings and the shift in consumer savings around the world out of bank deposits and into mutual funds. This field, therefore, presents exciting prospects for those who wish a career in it. I would advise students to assess their skills and ambitions to ensure they match the organization they wish to join. Organizational cultures vary among investment firms, and finding a firm with the proper fit is critically important for career success."

Careers in Investment Analysis

Jack S. Rader, CFA
Executive Director of Financial Management Association International,
Copyright © 1999, Financial Management Association International.
All rights reserved.

INTRODUCTION

The field of investment analysis can be broken down into two primary careers: security analyst and portfolio manager. Security analysts generally specialize in the evaluation of securities and other investments in asset classes such as equities, fixed income, real estate, or alternative assets. Portfolio managers work with (or for) individual investors or institutional investors, generally overseeing portfolios consisting of equities, fixed-income securities, other individual assets or multiple asset classes. Additionally, portfolio managers may be responsible for overlay strategies (such as risk or currency management).

Employment opportunities can be found with investment broker/dealer firms, mutual funds, investment banks, pension funds, foundations, trust and asset management departments of banks, independent asset management firms, and insurance companies. The positions available vary widely in responsibility and authority. Investment analyst positions offer individuals the opportunities to make decisions affecting many millions or billions of dollars, to execute the decisions, and to see the results of those decisions— good or bad—within a relatively short period of time. The pay can be extremely good— seven figure salaries are not out of the question—and the work is interesting.

A CLOSER LOOK AT INVESTMENT ANALYST CAREERS

The investment analyst profession is frequently divided into those who work on the buy-side and those who work on the sell-side. Security analysts and portfolio managers are said to work on the sell-side if they work for brokers/dealers, investment banks, or asset-management firms that do business by selling research, securities, or asset management services to investors and those who manage investor asset pools. Security analysts and portfolio managers are said to work on the buy-side if they are employed directly by investors (e.g., pension funds). The key to understanding the difference in buy-side and sell-side positions is fairly simple. Sell-side analysts and portfolio managers work for firms that make money selling securities and/or management services to investors. In short, they are responsible not only for research and management but also for developing new business. The clients of sell-side firms may be retail (individuals) or institutional (pension funds and other large institutional investors). Buy-side analysts and portfolio managers, on the other hand, are responsible not only for research and management but also for evaluating the usefulness of the products and services offered by the analysts and managers on the sell-side. That said, security analysts and portfolio managers on both sides perform very similar tasks. Complicating the picture somewhat is that a portfolio manager may function as a representative of a buy-side investor and yet be employed by a sell-side firm!

SECURITY ANALYSTS

The function of an equity research analyst is to assess the risks and expected returns of a company's stock. This entails analyzing a company's financial statements, researching the company and its industry (or industries), estimating a fair value for the stock, and preparing a report or recommendation as to whether the stock of the company is attractive or unattractive for purchase or retention in a portfolio. To do this, analysts use a number of analytical tools, talk to company management and research a number of other sources. Fixed income or bond analysts do much the same thing, except their focus is primarily on credit-worthiness and the factors that influence interest rate levels and trends. Real estate analysts and alternative asset analysts similarly adjust for the unique aspects of the asset classes they study.

A security analyst at a brokerage firm or other institutional sell-side firm typically specializes in only one or just a few industries, and is often considered an expert in the group or groups he or she follows (e.g., technology analyst, retail analyst). The job has three main responsibilities:

1) to analyze and stay current on the companies under his/her responsibility;
2) to disseminate this information and stock recommendations to the firm's clients; and,
3) to satisfy the investment needs of existing clients (i.e., keep them happy) and attract new clients to the firm.

Usually, the clients of an institutional sell-side analyst are buy-side analysts and portfolio managers. Sell-side analysts travel often, visiting the companies followed by their firms and calling on the buy-side clients. A sell-side analyst not only must be an expert on his or her stocks, but his or her information and advice must be timely, because many other investment professionals depend on this analysis as a valuable input to their investment decisions. Therefore, both analytical and communication skills are crucial, as is a willingness to sell the firm's services. Successful sell-side analysts gradually take on responsibility to represent their firms to clients, potential clients, and the investing public.

Buy-side analysts work closely with the portfolio managers in their organizations. Like sell-side analysts, they analyze, evaluate and recommend. The major differences are the direct link to the portfolios of investors and the lack of external sales responsibilities. Of course, there are still internal sales responsibilities in that the analyst's ideas have to be sold to the portfolio managers if they are to be implemented. On both the sell-side and the buy-side, good analysts become recognized as stores of knowledge and are frequently consulted by clients and coworkers in other areas of their organizations for their expertise.

PORTFOLIO MANAGERS

Using the insights of a number of security analysts, portfolio managers typically make the final decisions on whether to trade a security and then direct the trades. Portfolio managers tend to specialize in an asset class (e.g., stocks or bonds) or investment management style (e.g., growth stocks or value stocks). Portfolio management, however, is not just picking stocks and bonds. Particularly on the buy-side, determining appropriate investor objectives and constraints and establishing portfolio policies and strategies are an important part of the set of responsibilities, especially for senior portfolio managers. Also, portfolio managers need to integrate expectations for capital market risks and returns into the overall set of policies for a given portfolio.

Portfolio managers may be responsible for many other matters, as well. Risk management, external manager selection, performance evaluation, liquidity maintenance, tax management, currency management, and operational functions such as accounting and contracting might all be part of the job. Further, sell-side portfolio managers may have to attract new clients and keep current clients happy as do sell-side analysts.

OTHER POSITIONS

There are numerous other investment careers available that require specialized knowledge and expertise. Traders actually execute an organization's trades. Further, they may have authority to trade for the firm's account and thus serve as profit centers. Arbitrageurs attempt to "scalp" profits from small mispricings that might exist between, for example, a stock index and a futures contract. Risk arbitrageurs generally play suspected takeover targets, attempting to get in early before prices are bid up. Yet other opportunities exist in market or economic analysis, merger and acquisition analysis, credit analysis, investment banking, derivatives and financial engineering, real estate, and international investing. In fact, many specialty fields have developed and continue to develop as investment management techniques and financial markets and instruments continue to evolve.

EMPLOYERS

One important decision an aspiring investment analyst faces is whether to work on the buy-side or the sell-side.

Sell-Side Employers

Ultimately, sell-side employers sell research, trade execution and related record-keeping services, portfolio performance, asset-class or investment management style expertise, specialized services such as risk management overlays, and, to an extent, regulatory or legal insurance for fiduciaries who are involved in managing money on the buy-side. Following are descriptions of some of the organizations that are generally thought of as sell-side firms:

Broker/Dealers. Broker/dealers and other similar firms tend to offer "full service" investment counseling services, research, portfolio management, and other services. Additionally, they frequently trade for their own accounts. They can be exciting places to work and need sales representatives (e.g., account representatives), analysts, portfolio managers, and traders. These institutions manage tax-exempt portfolios such as pension funds, profit sharing funds, and endowment funds, but they also, in many cases, manage individuals' portfolios. Some of these firms are multi-national in scope; others are focused on regional or even local clients. Some firms are truly "full service" with extensive research and advice, and they charge relatively high fees that are attributable to the value of the services provided; others offer discounted services, low cost internet trading and less advice.

Investment Management Firms. A variety of firms offer buy-side clients a focused set of investment management products. These firms might be small shops with from one to ten employees or large financial firms with offices all over the world. The common thread is that the product is asset management; they provide portfolio management services in return for fees that range from a few basis points (in the case of a large institutional index fund provider) to perhaps 50-100 basis points (for more complex and specialized portfolios). The portfolio management products they offer range from commingled funds, which many different investors may use, to fully customized, stand-alone funds that are unique for a specific investor.

Pension Fund (and Other) Consultants. These firms generally offer neither fund management nor security analysis per se. What they offer is advice concerning: which portfolio management firms have done well and which have done poorly, which asset classes have had good risk/return performance and which have not, and so forth. Larger buy-side firms often turn to consultants to help them evaluate the offerings of sell-side firms.

Buy-Side Employers

The buy-side is comprised of a variety of financial institutions that manage money belonging to other people and institutions/investors that manage their own money. These institutions are the clients of sell-side firms. Their primary purpose is to manage money—their own or a principal on whose behalf they are acting (e.g., a pension fund which acts on behalf of plan beneficiaries and the plan sponsor). Following are descriptions of some of the organizations that are generally thought of as buy-side organizations:

Mutual Funds. These are pools of money representing the investments of many individual shareholders. Some mutual funds organizations have 20 or more funds and $100s of billions in assets; some individual funds have nearly $100 billion in assets. The typical mutual fund has a lead portfolio manager (sometimes a committee), a team of assistant portfolio managers, and support staff to handle investor relations, legal issues, and the like. The larger fund families have their own in-house analysts. Note that mutual funds sell their portfolio management services to retail (individual) and institutional clients and thus are also sell-side organizations.

Trust and Asset Management Departments of Banks. Trust departments take a somewhat longer view in terms of investment horizon than either investment counselors or mutual funds. Also, their work frequently involves other aspects of the trust business, such as estate planning. They tend to serve individuals and small businesses.

In recent years, larger banks have greatly expanded their trust operations into non-trust asset management. In doing so, they offer alternatives to the traditional broker/dealer firms as places of employment in a hybrid buy-side, sell-side environment. Very often, an entry-level investment analyst can receive some of the best training at a bank, starting as an assistant portfolio manager in a local office. Additionally, most larger banks have a team of analysts that serves the portfolio managers who in turn serve clients.

Insurance Companies. Insurance companies are not as well known as investors; in fact, however, they manage billions of dollars in investment portfolios. In life insurance companies, analysts or portfolio managers tend to focus heavily on bonds and real estate, because life companies are required by regulation to invest in a conservative manner. Property and casualty companies, on the other hand, invest a significant portion of their portfolio in common stocks.

Pension Funds. Pension funds are big investors with trillions of dollars under management. Some pension funds are defined-contribution and some are defined-benefit. All pension funds are complex organizations and need investment professionals. Correspondingly, they employ or cause to be employed, large numbers of security analysts and portfolio managers, as well as executives and administrators. Those that manage their assets internally need the full spectrum of specialized analysts and managers. Those that hire external managers still need skilled investment professionals to select and monitor those who manage the fund's money.

Foundations. A final, but not trivial, type of institutional investor is the foundation. These are operating entities that receive special tax treatment in order to pursue scientific, charitable, or educational activities. An endowment fund is an asset pool that provides the operating entity (e.g., a university) with funds to help it accomplish its mission. These asset pools can be quite large—in the billions of dollars for some foundations—and, as for pension funds, may be managed internally or externally.

CHOOSING AN EMPLOYER

For people who want to be on the sell-side, major financial centers such as New York, Boston, and Chicago are where most of the firms are located that hire sell-side analysts and portfolio managers (although there are several regional firms in other major cities, particularly on the retail side). This is not true for positions on the buy-side. Pension funds tend to be at corporate headquarters or state and local government centers. Foundations can be anywhere, and trust departments are everywhere. Mutual funds, of course, tend to cluster in the money center cities along with the sell-side organizations.

Aspiring investment analysts should try to find a firm or organization that provides a good training program. Hopefully, there will be opportunities to participate in and make investment decisions within a reasonably short period of time. Ideally, such a training program would be one in which junior employees are assigned to a senior investment professional from whom they can learn the business. The firm should support the Chartered Financial Analyst (CFA) program, and there should be a number of charterholders in the firm. Also, seek good visibility to others in the investment profession as well as the opportunity to observe other aspects of the investment business.

REQUIREMENTS FOR THE JOB

What talents and attributes are desirable in an investment analyst? In a speech given in 1981, Leon Cooperman, a Partner at Goldman Sachs and Co., (Careers In Finance, FMA, 1995) gave the following advice:

- *"Number one is to be analytical and insightful, not to be afraid of working with numbers, but rather to understand them and let them speak to you.*

- *Second is a high degree of persistence, a willingness to dig to get the difficult answers.*

- *Third is an ability to work with people.*

- *Fourth, and critical I think, is the ability to express oneself in writing."*

He goes on to add: *"You have to be a good salesperson. You have to get your ideas across; there is no value to a recommendation that is not executed."*

Today we should add that knowledge of computers is helpful. Further, we could argue that analysts have more to learn now than they did in 1981. Overall, however, Mr. Cooperman's advice seems as timely today as it was when he gave it.

CONCLUSION

Investment analysts need to be intellectually bright, hard working, and aggressive. They need to stay on top of a field that changes rapidly by continuing to learn. And, they need to understand that they are competing with equally bright, equally hard working people to find the best investment ideas, to get clients or to generate acceptable performance, and to add value to their employers.

Careers in investment analysis—as a security analyst, portfolio manager, or one of the numerous other positions that is available—can be interesting and exciting. Overall, investment analysis is challenging, fast-paced, vibrant, pressure-filled, and rewarding for those who do well. Is investment analysis right for you? Let's turn to Mr. Cooperman again for guidance:

"I think a person who wants to be right and is motivated to be the best in his or her field is very important. It's an extraordinarily competitive business. You should be aware there are a lot of people out there giving you a report card. Your mistakes are not hidden. Obviously, the market trades frequently, and your recommendations are up there on the tape. When you're right, it's a terrific feeling. When you're wrong, it's not terribly enjoyable. You have to take this business very seriously. If you come into it, recognize that you're very visible; you get a report card every day."

Mr. Cooperman's remarks are from a speech presented in 1981 at the NYSSA Career Day and reprinted with permission as *"Opportunities in Wall Street Research,"* Leon Cooperman, Partner, Goldman, Sachs, and Co. (*Careers in Finance, 1995,* Financial Management Association International, pgs.36-37).

Portions of this article are based on the article *"Careers in Investment Analysis,"* David J. McLaughlin, CFA Chase Investment Counsel Corporation, Formerly Vice President, Candidate Programs, ICFA (*Careers in Finance, 1995,* Financial Management Association International, pgs.23-24).

Focus on Careers: Becoming a Market Maker

The following article was developed by materials
provided with John Dempsey,
International Trading Institute, Ltd.
Reprinted by permission. Copyright © 1995.
All rights reserved.

INTRODUCTION

The market offers challenges and opportunities unsurpassed by almost any profession. The ability to generate substantial income while maintaining a level of independence creates a unique opportunity for the less risk-adverse, more skilled person.

Being self-employed, the Market-Maker has the challenges of operating a business and keeping pace with dynamic, explosive financial markets. The compensation, however, can be equally dynamic.

Market-Makers earn money based on their ability to calculate the value of options and make trades.   On a typical day at the Chicago Board of Options Exchange (CBOE), options worth several hundred million dollars will be traded. Not every trade will be profitable but, for the Money-Maker who can correctly predict the market and execute a trade, the earning potential is impressive. Unfortunately, so is the risk and thus the loss potential. A new Market-Maker, for example, who is adept, while learning the business can earn approximately $20,000 the first year. A less adept Market-Maker in training can lose an equivalent amount. The second year for the adept Market-Maker, $50,000 is a possibility and, as a trader becomes more experienced, there is no limit to what can be earned. For the less adept Market-Maker, of course, there may be no second year.

HOW TO GET STARTED

There is no such thing as a typical trader. In a recent survey of 20 new Market-Makers, their ages ranged from 23-54 and their level of education varied from high school to doctorate. Only one new Market-Maker had worked previously in the financial field. The only consistent quality among this diverse group was the desire to be a successful Market-Maker.

At the CBOE, one can apply for membership at 21 years of age. The necessary forms will be supplied. Included is your registration as a broker/dealer by the Securities and Exchange Commission, which generally takes 45 days to process.

Once registration is accepted, the candidate must pay an application fee, attend Exchange sponsored seminars and pass the membership examination. The exam is conducted once a month by the CBOE and may be taken up to three times if necessary. Once the exam has been passed, the candidate must be approved by the Exchange's membership committee.

Upon approval, the Market-Maker selects between two types of memberships: full and special. With a full membership, options can be traded on any equity, interest rate and index product that is offered on the Exchange. A special membership allows trading of options in a select number of stocks.

Prices for memberships fluctuate based on the state of the economy and the activity in the markets. A full membership may be leased of purchased; special membership is probably a better investment since, as a special member, the business can be learned with a minimum investment.

Once a membership has been purchased or leased, the member is given a floor badge. This badge allows the holder to enter the trading floor and operate as a Market-Maker.

Finally, although the Market-Maker operates as an independent businessperson, there are companies specially designed to assist in the trading process—the clearing firms. B|CBOE regulations require that an applicant have a clearing firm, to process and guarantee trades. A clearing firm is essentially a paperwork specialist, and, for its services, it charges the Market-Maker a small fee for every trade.

THE COST OF GETTING STARTED

While it is not excessively expensive to receive the training, become licensed, join a clearing firm, and obtain membership, capital is required to begin trading, to buy and sell contracts, and operate the business while still learning. A new Market-Maker should have approximately $20,000 to start.

EXPERIENCE IS THE BEST TEACHER

Becoming a Market-Maker is not the difficult part—being a Market-Maker is. To be successful, there are five primary skills to learn:

- How to make a market;
- How to trade;
- How to take a profit;
- How to take a loss;
- How to avoid the pitfall of trading.

How to Make a Market

When you make a market on an option you are stating the prices at which you are willing to buy and sell that option. As a Market-Maker, you have to create markets that the public will want to trade. At the same time, those markets should be profitable to you.

To effectively set your market, you must consider a number of questions:

- How does the stick's current price affect the option? Is the option "in-the-money," or "out-of-the-money?"

- How volatile is the stock?

- In how much time will the stock expire?

- What are the current interest rates and how will they affect the option?

If an option has more buyers than sellers, its market price will go up. Conversely, if an option has more sellers than buyers, its market price will decline. Therefore, Market-Makers use computer data, along with an understanding of the market forces, to set option prices.

Market-Makers announce the prices at which they are willing to trade their option by public outcry in the trading pit. Market-Makers set prices on more than one option at a time. When you make a market for an option on a stock, you are obligated to make markets for every option on that stock. That is part of your responsibility to the market. Your responsibility to yourself is to keep those markets current. As the stock price changes, your options prices should also change. It is an ongoing process. The Market-Maker who does not change his options prices to match the stock prices, can pay dearly for his inattentiveness.

How to Trade

If there are 2,000 Market-Makers at the CBOE, there are probably 2,000 ways to trade. Each trader had developed a style based on strategies and techniques with which he feels comfortable.

The most basic and common technique of trading is "scalping." This simply means buy low and selling high. Scalping requires that the trader be astute at making markets and filling orders of both buyers and sellers of options. If an option is frequently traded, a Market Maker can find it profitable to be a scalper.

However, not every option is frequently traded. An illiquid option presents a risk to the trader because a change in the stock's price could adversely affect the value of the option, and the Market-Maker can use a number of trading strategies to offset this risk. One technique is known as "spreading." A spread allows the trader to maintain a position, at limited or no risk, until it can be profitably sold.

To create a spread, the Market-Maker will sell another option or the stock to balance the risk of holding an illiquid option. It is important that the Market-Maker creates a spread at a fair or good price, so that the potential profit of the illiquid option is not lost. There are a number of spreading techniques that a Market-Maker can choose including: conversions, reversals, covered writes, vertical spreads, horizontal spreads, butterflies, backspreads, combinations, and straddles. The Market-Maker must decide which spread suits his trading strategy and the circumstances in which the options are trading.

Taking a Profit

When buying an option the Market-Maker should set a goal for the reasonable profit. If the opportunity to make that profit occurs the Market-Maker should take it without a second thought.

The most recurring lament heard on the trading floor is the profit that got away. The victim and the villain in this story are one and the same: the Market-Maker who did not take a profit when the opportunity arose. Whether the excuse was careless or greed, the consequence was the same—a small profit was traded for a big nothing.

Taking a Loss

A Market-Maker buys an option intending to sell it at a higher price. Of course, that might not happen. Once again, the important thing is to have a limit on what the Market-Maker is prepared to lose. If that limit is reached, the Market-Maker must be resolved to take that loss and get out of the position. By getting out of a losing position, the options are managing the Market-Maker.

How to Avoid the Pitfalls of Trading

There is actually only one pitfall the Market-Maker needs to be concerned with: a lack of discipline. It manifests itself in many ways.

A good trade is based on a price, a sound strategy and valid reasoning. A Market-Maker has an opinion, but it is important not to be opinionated; when the market changes, the market position of the trader should also change.

Also, every Market-Maker must find a level of activity that he is comfortable managing. That means not letting positions become too big or too complicated to manage.

The Market-Maker should not substitute wishful thinking for common sense; take a profit when you have it and take a loss while you can afford it.

For those who do not become greedy and can handle the volatility, being a Market-Maker is exciting and profitable. For the cautious, or the greedy, being a Market-Maker may not be a wise career choice.

Investment Management's Future

Harry S. Marmer, Director, Investment Management Services,
Frank Russell Canada Ltd. in Toronto.
Reprinted with permission from The Canadian Investment Review.
All rights reserved.

The investment management industry is impacted by many diverse forces: from technology and changing legislation to a continually changing market environment and a need to innovate to stay competitive. These were some of the issues addressed as the Toronto Society of Financial Analysts presented a forum on the "Future of the Investment Management Industry."

The forum drew sharp comparisons between the U.S. and Canada. In the U.S., assets in 401k and IRA accounts combined are significantly larger than assets in defined benefit funds (US$2.2 trillion vs. US$1.5 trillion). In addition, U.S., households have significantly increased the shares of financial assets invested in stocks and long bonds over the past 10 years. In contrast, Canada has yet to experience these trends. This suggests that there will be tremendous growth opportunities in the defined contribution market in Canada and that the Canadian retail market should grow in relative size and importance to the institutional market.

Industry concentration in Canadian retail and institutional markets is quite strong, as the top 10 managers in each of these markets manage a significant portion of assets (44% for the institutional market, and 61% for the mutual fund industry). This suggests that there is an attractive potential for new entrants, either Canadian or non-Canadian, who can effectively position new products and strategies. It also points out that Canadian managers in these top positions will need to sharpen product quality control if they are to maintain their alpha potential in a world of greater global competition.

THE EVOLUTION OF THE GLOBAL EQUITY MARKET

Jeffery Diermeier is managing partner, Brinson Partners in Chicago.

Managers need to adapt their organizations to the way they think securities will be priced from a global perspective. There are a number of reasons for this. First, production, marketing and distribution by multinationals has been globalized. Secondly, the European Monetary Union (EMU) is quickly moving us to a global economy. Increased disclosure has also awakened shareholder value globally.

Finally, the existence of an "irrational" home country bias provides managers with global opportunities. Home country bias is the tendency of investors to over invest locally, supporting market segmentation and causing "country effects" to exceed their true economic value. The opportunities for money managers lie in discovering processes to best take advantage of this inefficiency from a global perspective.

As we move towards this integrated market, we will not have a market of countries but rather a market of securities sensitive to a group of economic factors. These factors include industry factors, currency, country factors, stock specific factors and other common economic factors. In this world, currency management does not have a perfect solution. In addition, the move toward global integration will be challenged by major differences in international accounting. To help overcome these hurdles, research will have to split up across regions, where local research is then leveraged. The evolution of the global equity market will raise the ante for success for all money managers.

OPPORTUNITIES AND CHALLENGES

Roger Hertog, president and chief operating officer.
Sanford C. Bernstein & Company in New York.

Over the past 30 years the biggest change at the firm has been converting from a local investment manager to a global investment manager. The dominant theme in the future will be a far less robust and a more challenging investment environment manager. The recent real market returns are unsustainable as recent capital market returns have been in the experience of two or three standard deviation events on the upside (Table 1).

Table 1. U.S. Equity Returns

	1926-1998	1980-1998	1995-1998
Yield	4.7%	4.1%	2.8%
Growth	6.4	13.6	30.9
Total	11.1	17.7	33.7
Inflation	3.1%	4.2%	2.5%
Real Return	8.0	13.5	31.2

Source: Standard & Poors, Ibbotson Associates and Bernstein

People have significantly increased the amount they have in mutual funds, especially in equities. The mutual fund industry today in the U.S. is bigger than the banking industry from the perspective of who has the assets (Figure 1).

Figure 1. Mutual Fund Growth

Mutual funds have grown substantially, both in assets and breadth of ownership.

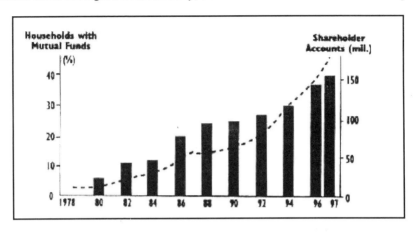

Table 2. Composition of Household Financial Assets

Directly Held Securities	20%
Banking and Thrifts	35 %
Mutual Funds	35%
Other	10%

For the bottom 80% of the income distribution

Source: Federal Reserve Board and Bernstein estimates

People have invested much more in mutual funds because they believe they are less risky and the returns in the market are much better than the other investments. The result is that people's expectations for markets are overblown.

Table 3. Unrealistic Expectations

When asked, "How will the market in the future perform, compared to the 14% annual return in the past decade?" the responses were:

Perform the same	56%
Perform better	29%
Perform Worse	14%
Don't know	2%

Source: Lou Hams & Associates

Given the potential for information overload, and the significant portion that equities occupy on the individual balance sheet, the key question is how individual investors will react when we have a two-standard deviation event on the downside.

As the individual investor continues to grow in importance from both purchasing power and percentage of invested assets in the market, investment management industry leaders will need to invest in the systems to help these investors make efficient after-tax investment decisions. There is no question that the next bear market will help to rationalize the industry for the benefit of all consumers, especially individuals.

COMPETITION IN THE INVESTMENT MANAGEMENT INDUSTRY

Richard Ennis is principal, Ennis Knupp & Associates in Chicago.

The investment industry has become a marketing industry but its future will be dependent on textbook economics. Market efficiency can range from grossly inefficient to perfectly efficient. Industry structure as well can range from a concentrated to a highly segmented industry. The industry structure theorem states that the investment management industry is as concentrated as the level of information concentration.

In the U.S., the active investment industry is unconcentrated as well as unstable. This means that the leaders in one period are not the leaders in the next period. There has also been a substantial contraction in the number of managers in the industry (Figure 2). The key reason for these changes over time has been that assets pursue performance and there is little evidence of performance persistence.

The passive industry is a classic oligopoly. It is a concentrated industry with a stable market share, with undifferentiated products and marginal costs near zero. There are incentives for clients to consolidate with a single firm. Economies of scale create barriers to entry for new firms. In addition, indexing has been consistently growing as a percentage of market share.

Figure 2. Number of Managers Contracting

The number of tax-exempt "active" asset managers has declined during the decade in the U.S.

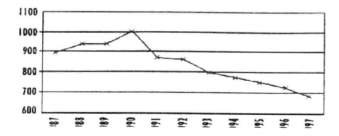

Source: Pension & Investments

Growth in our assets under management has been explosive. For example, while the country's real GDP has increased 88%, real increase in demand for active management has increased 600% over the past 22 years.

Over the same period, we have seen a shift in resource allocation from resource to product development, marketing and professional client service. Firms have also increased the number of products that they offer, for the simple reason that the more products you have the higher the probability of marketing success. Efficient markets drive firms to become multi-product providers. Unfortunately, clients and consultants are overwhelmed by the number of products.

The greatest opportunity in investment management is in segmented markets. There are many sources of segmentation including taxation, liquidity, international factors, legal restrictions, multiple classes of shares and risk tolerance. A key indicator of a segmented market is aggregate benchmark ambiguity, which means that the experts cannot agree upon a universal market index for the investment class. The two prominent examples of this are fixed income and international equities.

For active managers the greatest threat is indexing, with a forecast of up to 50% of the market eventually being indexed. Indexing, for all the reasons noted, will become an industry of only four or five firms. For active managers, the key strategy will revolve around product development marketing, while strong relationships will continue as a vital strategy.

INVESTMENT MANAGEMENT A DECADE FROM NOW

Lloyd Atkinson is principal, Perigee Investment Counsel Inc. in Toronto.

Consolidation will continue to occur in both the institutional and retail markets. The result is that size will matter. Large money managers with multiple styles will be the direction of the future. Increased competition will change how we service and market to clients. Fee pressures will be brought on by the largest of buyers.

The context for the future is that we are living through a technology revolution, much like the industrial revolution. The driver will be higher productivity and consequently, substantial improvements in wealth. Technology will allow investment firms to continue to build multiproduct businesses. Part and parcel of this new environment is ongoing, long-term low inflation. The bottom line is that the monetary authorities have outlawed money supply growth. Deficit growth will continue to slow which will continue to bring down real interest rates.

Corporations are continuing to examine the defined contribution market, which will lead the institutional industry to take on a more retail look. Increased competition, especially from the U.S. market, will continue to intensify. New market opportunities will be especially strong in Japan and Europe.

The Investment Management Industry Food Chain

Keith Ambachtsheer is president, KPA Advisory Services in Toronto.

Let's examine, from an economic perspective, how the ideal investment industry should function. The ideal investment industry should have the following characteristics:

1. Efficient capital markets;

2. Recognition that investment costs can significantly impact terminal wealth; and,

3. Informational symmetry between customers and suppliers, i.e., "win-win" outcomes for customers and suppliers.

This context suggests the following:

1. A high proportion of assets are indexed;

2. A low proportion of assets are actively managed; and,

3. Investment performance is measured net of fees relative to invisible benchmarks.

In reality we do not find this type of market. Why do we have such a gap between the ideal and the actual where, using the metaphor of a food chain, the suppliers are on top and the customers are on the bottom? This is especially the case in the retail sector. The main reason for this gap is that informational symmetry does not exist. In other words, buyers lack an understanding of:

1. How scarce successful active management is; and,

2. The impact of fees on accumulating investment wealth.

This gap will narrow for a number of reasons including:

1. The profile of these issues is rising;

2. The institutional buy-side is starting to achieve a better balance between adopting the analysis of value and the cost of production;

3. A single-digit return world will soon reappear; and

4. Both buyers and sellers are responding to this "ideal-actual" gap in the market by devising new strategies to reduce this gap.

The Retail Financial Services Industry

Earl Bederman is president, Investor Economics in Toronto.

The key to understanding the retail market is to examine the household balance sheet. It is clear that financial assets have substituted for deposits and that is where the opportunities lie.

There are several themes within the retail market. Total assets are growing, but at a slower rate than in the past. In addition, there is a shift from short-term to long-term funds which also reduces the liquidity of their balance sheet.

Part of the solution here is to provide international products for diversification. This means that Canadian money managers will need to gear up for the challenge of foreign managers who enter the Canadian marketplace to satisfy consumer demand.

Taxable assets should also continue to grow in significance, relative to non-taxable assets. This trend will be reinforced by growing consumer awareness of the importance of after-tax returns and the return of the single-digit return era.

The growth in investment funds has resulted in over 1,500 funds available today in Canada. The shift from transactions to fee-based products over the past five years has been enormous. Financial institutions see this as a gateway to providing advisory services to clients. In the U.S., 70% of individual assets are in long-term risky assets. This stands in sharp contrast to Canada, where about 50% of assets are in risky assets.

Stockbroker

Reprinted with permission, The Princeton Review, Guide to Your Career.
Copyright 1996, 1997, 1998, Princeton Review Publishing, L.L.C.
www.review.com

A DAY IN THE LIFE (CAREER PROFILE)

A stockbroker invests in the stock market for individuals or corporations. Only members of the stock exchange can conduct transactions, so whenever individuals or corporations want to buy or sell stocks they must go through a brokerage house. Stockbrokers often advise and counsel their clients on appropriate investments. Brokers explain the workings of the stock exchange to their clients and gather information from them about their needs and financial ability, and then determine the best investments for them. The broker then sends the order out to the floor of the securities exchange by computer or by phone. When the transaction has been made, the broker supplies the client with the price. The buyer pays for the stock and the broker transfers the title of the stock to the client and performs clearing and settlement procedures. The beginning stockbroker's first priority is learning the market. One broker said, "First you have to decide whether you have an interest in the stock market. This will determine how well you'll do. If you're just interested in making money you won't get very far." Stockbrokers spend their time in a fast-paced office, usually working from nine to five, unless they are just starting out or have to meet with clients. The new broker spends many hours on the phone building up a client base. Sometimes brokers teach financial education classes to expose themselves to potential investors who may then become their clients.

PAYING YOUR DUES (MAJOR EMPLOYERS)

A college degree is not required, but most brokers have one. Brokers have to be licensed. A license is obtained by passing the General Securities Registered Representative Examination and, in many cases, posting a bond. Individuals may take this test after they have been employed by a brokerage firm for four months. Firms use these four months as an on-the-job training period to prepare their workers for the test. Many states also require the candidate to take the Uniform Securities Agents State Law Examination. These tests are designed to ensure the candidate's knowledge of all aspects of the stock market. After passing these tests, an individual is considered a trainee. While working full-time, he takes classes and trains for up to two years. Employees are expected to take training courses throughout their careers to keep abreast of developments in the field. Those with prior work experience have the greatest opportunities for becoming a stockbroker. Few people become brokers straight out of college. Most employers seek applicants who have already succeeded in other fields, such as insurance sales. If you know your interests lie in the market, study economics, finances, computers, and business management in college. Many employers view ambition as the most important quality a candidate can possess.

Associated Careers (Who You'll Work With)

The sales aspects and the need to build up a client base are similar for stockbrokers and insurance and real estate agents. Financial planners create and execute financial plans for people or businesses. They ascertain their clients' needs, resources and goals and use this information to draw up a financial plan that suits the individual or the company. Traders are the people you see in the movies yelling on the chaotic floor of the stock exchange. They perform the actual exchanges.

Past and Future (Major Associations)

The stock market is strongly affected by economic boom-and-bust cycles, the most famous of which occurred in October 1929—the Great Crash—causing a large number of investors to leap out of the windows of their offices on Wall Street. The industry has matured a great deal since then—now Wall Street offices have sealed upper-floor windows and the markets have automatic limits on how far average stock prices can rise or fall in a given session—but historically only those brokers with iron stomachs have survived in this high-risk, high-stakes industry. The outlook for stockbrokers is rosy, as economic growth is anticipated. Deregulation of the industry is allowing many stockbrokers to expand their responsibilities, bringing about a corresponding increase in their client base. Increased concern about financing pension plans is also causing many people to turn to stockbrokers for advice, and the stock market continues to attract increasing numbers of individual investors. However, this is a boom-or-bust business, so the upswing won't last forever.

Quality of Life

Two Years Out: Stockbrokering is an extremely competitive business—perhaps the most competitive of all. There is heavy burnout in the early years due to outrageous hours—all-nighters are routine occurrences for eager and ambitious upstarts—and many novice brokers fail to establish an adequate client base early on. Those that stay find the work exciting but anxiety-provoking. There is greater security in larger companies but generally a longer wait for advancement and "the big bucks."

Five Years Out: Those who get through the first few rocky years tend to stay in the field for an extended period. Many find the high salaries a delicious payback for those first years spent toiling "in the trenches." Leaving for an MBA is common at this point for those who want to return for top management positions in the industry.

Ten Years Out: At this point brokers are enjoying the fruits of their extensive and intensive education and training. Advancement in this field comes in the form of more and bigger accounts or management positions. Occasionally, it culminates in partnership in the firm. Some even retire at this point, but most like the industry and stick around for years after they've earned pots of money.

CAREER PROFILE

# of people in profession:	250,000
% male	85
% female:	15
average hours per week:	40
average starting salary:	$ 17,000
average salary after 5 years:	$ 30,000
average salary after 10 to 15 years:	$ 65,000

PROFESSIONALS READ:

Wall Street Journal, Institutional Investor, Financial Executive Journal

BOOKS, FILMS AND TV SHOWS FEATURING THE PROFESSION:

Wall Street, Bonfire of the Vanities, Liar's Poker, Trading Places

MAJOR EMPLOYERS:

J.P. Morgan
60 Wall Street
New York, NY 10260
Tel: 212-483-2323
Fax: 212-648-5177
Contact: Human Resources

Barclays Capital
222 Broadway
New York, NY 10038
Tel: 212-412-4000
Fax: 212-412-6795
Contact: Human Resources

YOU'LL ASSOCIATE WITH:

Clients, Financial Analysts, Stock Traders, Researchers

MAJOR ASSOCIATIONS:

Securities Industry Association
120 Broadway
New York, NY 10271
Tel: 212-608-1500
Fax: 212-732-6096
Contact: Human Resources

American Financial Services Association
919 18th Street, NW
Washington, DC 20006
Tel: 202-296-5544
Fax: 202-223-0321
Contact: Human Resources

Association for Investment Management and Research
PO Box 3668
Charlottesville, VA 22903
Tel: 804-977-6600
Fax: 804-963-6842
Contact: Human Relations Department

INSURANCE

Career Opportunities in Insurance

Dr. Dale A. Johnson, Associate Professor of Finance
University of South Florida

Dr. Johnson received a DBA in Finance and Insurance from Georgia State University. He is a licensed property and casualty agent in Florida and has worked as a commercial property and casualty underwriter for several years. He frequently consults as an expert witness in legal cases involving insurance. He also holds the CPA designation.

INTRODUCTION

This article examines several of the career opportunities which are available to individuals interested in insurance and related fields. The first section discusses sales positions in life and property and casualty insurance; the second section looks at underwriting, investments, claims, computer-related, loss prevention, and the actuarial sciences as career alternatives to the more well-known "sales" position.

SALES

Life Insurance

Traditionally, the position with life insurers that has been the most widely available of, interviewed for, has been for life and health insurance sales. This is still the case; however, the positions have expanded to include other aspects of financial planning for the client. A life insurance sales position entails the marketing of various types of policies such as term, whole-life, and universal life, as well as individual retirement accounts and other products and services related to financial planning.

There are licensing requirements in most, if not all, states for life agents. In Florida, for instance, a 40-classroom-hour course has to be completed before sitting for the life agent's licensing exam. The course is conducted by insurers, private schools, and universities. In addition to the life agent's license, a securities dealer's license may also be required if the product sold involve other than just the life insurance contracts.

The income potential in life insurance is up to the individual. Many companies will pay a salary or provide a draw against commissions during a training period; however, most life agents are paid strictly on a commission basis. An exception may be in the area of group sales where individuals who specialize in the marketing of group life and health insurance may be paid a salary rather than just commissions.

A good agent will make money. While the income potential is up to the individual, incomes in the range of $100,000 per year are not unusual after a few years. There are some caveats. To be successful as a life agent, the person has to be willing to work long hours that may be irregular; must be highly motivated; and, must have the ability to face rejection.

The successful life agent must also be well-trained and professional. Indications of the level of competence can be found in the professional designations that an agent may acquire. The most common is the CLU (Chartered Life Underwriter) designation. To receive this designation, a person must pass a series of ten two-hour examinations. The degree of difficulty is comparable to the CPA exams. A newer designation is the ChFC (Chartered Financial Consultant). This also involves ten exams, but since there is an overlap with the CLU exams, both designations can be obtained by passing 12 exams in total. There is also a graduate designation available - the Masters in Financial Services— through the American College. Another designation is the CFP (Certified Financial Planner), which emphasizes the broader aspects of financial planning.

Property and Casualty

The other primary sales positions in insurance are in the area of property and casualty insurance. A position in property and casualty sales is more difficult to find than one in life and health for a variety of reasons. One reason is that many companies prefer the person applying for a property and casualty position to have other sales experience or be more mature as far as age is concerned. Another reason is the licensing requirement. In Florida, for example; one way to become eligible to sit for the property and casualty (general lines) licensing exam is to complete a 240-classroom-hour course requirement. This coursework may be offered by insurers, private schools, universities (both traditional coursework and continuing educational programs), and community colleges. A person may also become eligible to sit for the exam through work experience of one year; however, the pass ratio amount of those using work experience is not high.

If a person gets past the licensing requirements, the income potential is comparable to that of a life agent. The degree of difficulty in making the income is comparable also, but varies depending upon whether one specializes in personal lines of coverage or commercial lines of coverage. With personal lines, the customer is more likely to come to the agent than with life insurance. For commercial lines, the business is more competitive; the agent has to do a better selling job.

As with the life and health area, the successful general lines agent is knowledgeable and professional. The primary professional designation in the area is the CPCU (Chartered Property and Casualty Underwriter) designation. It also requires the passing of ten two-hour exams and is comparable in difficulty to the CPA exams.

ALTERNATIVES TO SALES

So far, the only careers mentioned in insurance have been in sales. There are many other career areas in insurance which can be interesting and satisfying. These include, but are not limited to, underwriting, investments, accounting, claims adjusting, data processing, loss prevention, and statistical and actuarial. These areas are not limited to positions with insurers but may also include positions with agencies such as the Insurance Commissioner's Office, consulting firms and independent adjusting firms.

Underwriting

Underwriting involves the selection and pricing of business acceptable to the company. The underwriter is usually a salaried person whose job is primarily in an office. In the life and health area, the term underwriter is often used to refer to someone in a sales position; often, however, this term applies to the office position relating to the acceptance or rejection of business. In the general lines area, the underwriter may be in the personal lines or in the commercial lines. Quite often the underwriting offices for personal lines and commercial lines are located in different cities. While both lines can be challenging, commercial lines are more so. The commercial underwriter has to have a thorough knowledge of the contracts offered, the rating plans available, and a feel for which prospects represent less loss exposure to the company. The CPCU designation is usually desirable in an underwriting position. The income potential in underwriting is probably less than in sales, until the person reaches the supervisory ranks. A degree in business administration is desirable; however most companies look just as favorably on a liberal arts degree. Most companies that actively recruit for underwriting positions have in-house training programs. Many companies have a mix of formal and on-the-job training. These programs last 6 months to 1 year. It can take several years to become a competent underwriter.

Investments

For the finance major, the insurance industry offers many opportunities in the investments area. Insurers represent a very important financial institution with positions available for the management of their investments. To illustrate, the life insurance industry alone holds assets well in excess of one trillion dollars. In addition, the property and casualty insurers hold roughly half of the amount in the same types of assets. They consist of government securities, corporate bonds and stocks, mortgages, real estate, and other investments.

Accounting

For accounting majors, there are positions in general accounting areas and in the area of auditing of exposure for premium determination and loss auditing. These positions involve a fair amount of travel with the opportunity to visit many of the policyholders' facilities. While that may not lead to a further career in insurance, it may lead to a career with a policyholder.

Positions are also available for accounting majors with the various State

Commissioner's offices. This typically involves examination of insurers and the financial statements they file with the commissioners.

Claims

The claims adjuster's position can vary from the routine, where most work is done in the office, to the very complex. Positions are available with both insurers and independent adjusters have training programs; the knowledge required of the underwriters—a thorough knowledge of the contracts. These positions are generally salaried positions, with a car or expenses if travel is involved. A caveat for the person who considers claims adjusting as a career—the persons in the managerial positions quite often have legal training. Without legal training, the potential for advancement may be limited.

Data Processing

As with most industries, the insurance industry has become more and more computerized. For the person whose background or interest lies in computers, there are numerous opportunities in the industry, from company operations to underwriting software programs.

Loss prevention

Loss prevention involves an attempt to reduce the frequency of severity of losses through recommendations to policy holders. This area also provides opportunities for persons trained in health-related fields such as nursing, medicine, and chemistry to work with the hazardous products such as chemicals. Loss prevention usually requires some technical or engineering training. These positions involve a lot of travel and are usually salaried.

Statistical and Actuarial

The statistical and actuarial areas are specialized positions which rely heavily on a math background. Formal programs in actuarial science are limited in number. For example, the only university in the southeast that offers a degree in actuarial sciences is Georgia State University in Atlanta.

The actuary is involved with statistical work, rate-making for all lines, pensions and profit-sharing plans. Much actuarial work is done by independent consulting firms. For the person with a math orientation, actuaries are salaried and well-paid. It would not be unusual for someone with a bachelor's degree in actuarial science to start at over $30,000 with considerably more after two to three years.

SUMMARY

As can be seen, there are many career opportunities in insurance. Some require specialized backgrounds other than business administration. Many though, are available to, and can offer challenging and rewarding opportunities for the graduate in business administration. Many of these positions are not actively recruited on campuses, but are available.

Career Opportunities in Real Estate

Dr. Waldmar M. Goulet, Professor of Finance,
Wright State University and
Marcia Loderman, Graduate Assistant
Copyright © 1999, Financial Management Association International.
All rights reserved.

Opportunities in finance and those ancillary areas relating to the field of finance have grown over the past two decades. Of all the business areas, students majoring in finance are finding that there are many directions in which they may prepare themselves for job placement opportunities. One of the older, related areas is that which this article is about, careers in real estate.

TYPES OF JOBS

The following is a partial listing of career options available to those interested in real estate. The more esoteric types of jobs such as real estate law, real estate appraisal and specialized fields of real estate finance, such as syndicating, are not discussed in order to concentrate on the broader career options available in real estate. Additional detailed information can usually be found in your library or by writing to one of several professional organizations.

Salesperson

Real estate sales is a good job to begin gaining broad experience in the field of real estate. Salespeople are employed by brokers and also act as agents. Their main job is to match a buyer's needs with listings. This consists of obtaining leads, attracting buyers, and handling all preliminary aspects of the sales negotiations. A salesperson generally splits the commission with the broker. Earnings for experienced salespersons may be $20,000 or more and are mainly commission based on sales. However, sometimes there are salaried employees. The individual salesperson must be licensed by the state.

Brokers

A broker is an individual or firm, which employs salespeople. In this position, additional managerial talents are required, as a broker must manage people, operations and finances. Their compensation comes from the listings and/or sales passing through their firm. Brokers must be licensed by the state.

Mortgage Manager

This involves obtaining loan information, analyzing risk and assigning the appropriate interest rate and lending term. Since this job still offers the opportunity to visit some of the sites, it is not truly a desk job. Although usually a salaried position, there is often an opportunity to earn a bonus.

Property Manager

A property manager is frequently a corporate executive who is responsible for all facets of apartment operations (for example, marketing, accounting, financing, leasing, securing of tenants, etc.). It is an exciting and interesting job that enables finance majors to apply all of the fields studied in business administration. The property management firm earns its fees either from a fixed charge or from a percent of the net rents; employees are normally salaried.

Urban Planning

An urban planner conducts practical research regarding land usage and development, and for larger cities, may work with land use trends and suggest rezoning and/or rehabilitation in order to efficiently utilize the land. This position is salaried. It may be contractual in the case where a consultant is utilized.

TYPES OF AGENCIES OR ORGANIZATIONS

Each of the institutions discussed below has a particular asset composition reflecting the nature of its operations, liabilities, tax considerations, and legal constraints. Some of the functions are common among types of organizations and hence, when one prepares professionally, the talents acquired may be utilized in a number of different environments.

Brokerage Offices

Most brokerage firms are small in size although there are large real estate firms in major cities that may be a part of a national franchise organization. Office space is normally provided regardless of the size of the brokerage operations; equipment and clerical staff are typically available for administrative support. These firms generally offer maximum opportunities for independent entrepreneurial growth.

Industrial and Commercial Operations

Many large firms, such as Mead Paper and the Chrysler Corporation have a real estate function within their organization. The individual is employed by the firm, yet his or her activities are concerned with the primary real estate needs of the firm (such as site locations for K-Mart Stores).

Commercial Banks and Saving and Loan Associations

Some purists may take umbrage at the linking of these two types of institutions; nonetheless, with recent changes in the federal regulations of financial institutions, the distinction is blurring. These institutions specialize in lending monies to potential purchasers of residential or business properties. Many of the jobs listed above are available in these types of firms.

Federal Agencies

The Federal Home Loan Bank Board offers opportunities that are more research oriented than those of many other institutions. For example, they publish a newsletter dealing with sales prices, interest rates, loan terms, etc. These institutions offer challenging positions to those who are interested in learning about real estate finance from a macro perspective.

Mortgage Brokers and Bankers

These firms serve as liaison between a potential mortgagee and mortgagor. These companies are continually looking for sources of funds to lend and for potential investors who have borrowing needs. These companies usually have small offices with a high dollar volume of business. Mortgage brokers do not service loans, whereas, mortgage bankers do service loans. Hence, in severe economic downturns, security of employment is generally higher at mortgage banking firms.

State and City Governmental Organizations

Many cities and states operate an urban planning section or real estate analysis department because these governmental agencies own property. There are two reasons for their owning property: (1) for their own administrative use; and (2) because of default on property taxes. Opportunities in these types of governmental positions encompass not only urban planning but also typical real estate activity (e.g., negotiation with firms to purchase properties, which have been defaulted to the city or state.)

TYPES OF REAL ESTATE (BUSINESS AREAS)

Residential Brokerage

A residential broker sells clients' residential property and must be familiar with the local residential market. This area of real estate is a good place for an individual to learn the fundamental characteristics of zoning regulations, property taxes, building codes and property values.

Industrial Brokerage

An industrial broker helps to determine good development locations for particular industries. It is mandatory that this type of broker understands what factors satisfy the needs of an organization. For example, a firm might want to consider availability

71

of education facilities, types of labor, and transportation.

Farm Brokerage

Another area of real estate requiring expertise is farm brokerage. Because these brokers act in an intermediary capacity between those buying and selling agricultural real estate, they should have technical experience in areas of irrigation systems, tax laws dealing with farm, production costs and agricultural economics.

Acreage

Many brokerage firms specialize in the sale of acreage (i.e., large expanses of vacant land). Generally, these firms have studied the potential land use and are familiar with the physical, legal and political factors affecting the land they are attempting to list and to sell.

EDUCATIONAL REQUIREMENTS

There is a wide range of educational requirements, which extend from a minimum of high school to an advanced degree (e.g., law) which may be necessary for the various types of real estate positions. Even when the minimum academic requirement is a high school diploma, most states require professional coursework before the state licensing exam is given. Some states are considering a degree in rea estate as a prelicensing requirement while other states mandate six to eight professional courses relating to real estate functions. In order to minimize the total number of courses needed to secure a position in any of the types of real estate jobs, students majoring in finance or real estate should investigate the laws of the state wherein they wish to be employed.

Commercial Banking: The Career Path and Preparation

David F. Scott, Jr., President, FMA, 1985-1986;
Executive Director, Dr. Phillips Institute for the Study of American Business Activity;
Holder, Phillips-Scheck Chair in American Private Enterprise and
Professor of Finance, University of Central Florida
Copyright © 1999, Financial Management Association International.
All rights reserved.

ORIENTATION

Commercial banking and financial institutions in general, are always in the forefront of business literature. The prominent role that these intermediaries play in the transfer of savings into ultimate investment is well known and studied in great depth. It is also no secret that business schools like to cultivate strong and positive relationships with commercial banks and other depository institutions. Financial corporations hire a significant number of business school graduates. For the same reason, banks have a vested interest in the nation's schools of business. These colleges are supposed to produce a graduate who can enter the banking establishment and have a net positive impact on the output of the institution. Such mutual interest is stressed in this article.

The thoughts contained herein are intended for (1) students considering a career in commercial banking or within other depository institutions, (2) professors who both teach and counsel business students, and (3) those educators who are involved with curriculum issues. Initially, we focus on a successful college graduate training program in place at Barnett Bank (headquarters, Jacksonville, Florida) to describe how one financial institution develops its human resources and advances them through the early phases of their careers. The description is brief, but will give students a sense of what occurs after they graduate and find themselves inside the banking organizations.

Next, we discuss from the perspective of the bank what type of student is being sought as a trainee. This involves a discussion of a university curriculum and its components. You will find that Barnett stresses some areas and courses not always dwelled upon by business educators. Further, we emphasis what the student can actually do through choice of major and thoughtful use of elective courses to enhance his or her job-market appeal. Last, in the conclusion, we put forth some value judgements aimed at finance educators.

THE CAREER PATH IN COMMERCIAL BANKING

Barnett Bank is a mid-sized multi-bank holding company headquartered in Florida with consolidated assets exceeding $14.8 billion at the end of 1985. Typically, Barnett hires College graduates with business degrees and places them in an extensive 15-18 month training program. This program encompasses specific training in (1) commercial loan analysis, (2) loan compliance and documentation, and (3) bank operations. At the end of the training program, the Commercial Track Management Associates (MA) usually become lending assistants to commercial lenders for about six months. At this point, MA is typically promoted to a junior lending position and given limited lending authority.

Next, the individual receives one to four years of direct line experience. At the conclusion of this stage, there is an offer of expanded opportunities with supervisory duties. The individual may take over a branch bank running the day–to–day operations and attending to all the commercial solicitation and borrowing needs of the surrounding community. Other possibilities include moving into corporate banking positions as corporate loan officer, cash management representative, or some other position. The individual could also advance within his or her original line position. Here the task is to develop other junior lenders, who are beginning their careers.

All of these paths entail gaining some particular specialty in the early stages of career development. What is emphasized is that the employee must become proficient, in a most-precise sense, in a given area of banking. Generalities are left behind and accomplishments are crucial to advancement. Most opportunities also provide exposure to supervisory relationships, managing a business unit with budgetary control, personnel management, customer interaction, the design of marketing objectives, and the other dynamic entities of any business. Some mixture of all these areas, plus management of the commercial credit deportment or involvement in loan administration, can be experienced during the course of a career.

Upon demonstrating for an extended period of time the line, supervisory, and other skills needed to successfully plan, coordinate, and run a business unit, the individual is in a position to move into (lower-level) senior management positions. These include senior vice presidential or higher positions. The employee would often head up a departmental function such as real estate lending, cash management, loan administration, or oversee commercial lending operations in a given county or other region.

While the possibilities outlined here relate directly to Barnett Bank, they are similar to career paths at other mid-sized commercial banks. College recruits for commercial lending and corporate services related functions of mid-sized and large banks would generally receive some specialized training. They will then go into a line, or other function, and based upon achievements move upward through the organization.

ENHANCING YOUR CHANGES OF SUCCESS IN COMMERCIAL BANKING: CURRICULUM VERSATILITY—THE KEY TO FLEXIBILITY

A career in commercial banking requires rigorous training to be successful and to fit the specialized needs of commercial banks. Usually financial institutions look for individuals with degree-majors in one of the following areas: finance, accounting, economics, management, or marketing.

While these degrees are acceptable, there are many things that students can do to enhance his or her chances for an entry-level position in commercial banking. Such enhancements serve as a springboard to ultimate success in any business-related position. Based on today's banking industry needs, you will find recommendations of minimum curriculum standards that should be met in various disciplines.

Communication

This is mentioned first, because it is truly important and is often not required or is under-emphasized in the standard business curriculum. Commercial banking relies extensively on written and oral communication skills. The employee must have these skills to successfully negotiate with customers, loan committees, and internal auditors. Writing skills are needed to prepare loan documentation and policy recommendations. Community relations and the business social circle depend on communication skills.

A minimum of three or four courses that deal with communications should be taken in the curriculum. The course work should include (1) at least once class in report writing, (2) one class in oral presentations, and (3) one class that combines a mixture of oral and written presentations on the same topic. These classes are in addition to normal business classes that require oral and written presentations. The objective is to teach the techniques of written and oral presentations. Of some benefit are classes in new report writing taught in journalism departments and debate classes taught in speech or humanities departments.

Finance

Achievement in commercial banking hinges on accurate and thorough analysis of corporations and an assessment of the financial risks associated with those firms. Being able to competently analyze corporate financial statements will provide the student with an edge both in landing a job and also in being successful.

We recommend that a minimum of four finance-related courses should be taken. These include (1) courses that acquaint the student with the financial environment (markets and competition), (2) financial structure design (corporate finance) and (3) financial statement analysis. Work in corporate taxation and tax strategies is especially beneficial if it can be taken near graduation. In some schemes this type of class may fall under the accounting discipline. Exposure to use of the personal computer is presumed here.

Accounting

A useful financial analysis is dependent on the accounting principles, techniques, and assumptions that go into building the reporting statements that financially describe all of business. Additionally, no matter what career path in business is sought, ultimate success will bring with it involvement in budgets and accounting reporting issues. These will affect the way in which the practitioner handles business. It is for these reasons that there is no substitute for a thorough knowledge of accounting. With the exception of principle classes, its importance is sometimes overlooked.

A minimum of four courses in accounting is recommended. These include classes in principles plus additional classes in managerial and cost accounting. Additionally, advanced accounting and auditing are highly desirable. Barnett, and some other banks, typically will not hire a commercial lending trainee without a minimum of 12 semester hours of accounting.

Economics

Business cycles and business conditions analysis are fascinating topics. A systematic knowledge of business cycles can minimize the chance of company failure and enhance the output of even the most competent management. From the bank's perspective it is crucial to understand the nature of economic cycles, understand the global economic environment, and relate this knowledge to the activities of the financial institution. Adequate preparation requires two courses in economic principles (these should stress macro concepts, micro concepts, and comparative systems). Our preference extends to at least one added course in business cycle analysis.

Business Law

Business law is one of the most difficult subjects and is prone to constant change and revision. For these reasons, it is recommended to delay taking business law classes until the end of one's school career if at all possible. A minimum of two courses is assumed. The emphasis should be on commercial contract law and the Uniform Commercial Code.

Management

The importance of management is universal. A well-managed bank depends on effective management skills. Management skills are difficult to teach, but the attempt must be made. Understanding how large-scale organizations fit the pieces together and arrive at decisions must be examined and learned. Three courses are suggested.

Humanities

Although the humanities do not apply directly to commercial lending, this grouping has significant value in the form of understanding people, developing empathy for people and exercising common sense. Business transactions require dealing with people. You have to understand clients, relate to them, and ultimately provide them a service that is of economic benefit. Humanities classes can provide a base to help in achieving these goals.

Extracurricular

Extracurricular activities enhance the student's chances for entry-level positions and simultaneously help build skills for long-run success. Commercial banks are searching for active individuals that will become involved in their communities. This not only serves as an obvious starting point for the solicitation of business, but also enhances the bank's reputation and standing in the community. Realize that banks can be under tremendous social pressures when, in the course of business, they have to foreclose on a "desirable organization or individual." They are exposed to continuous media attack. Therefore, it is necessary that the bank's personnel stay active in the community and represent the bank as a good neighbor to the community.

CONCLUSION: SOME THOUGHTS FOR FINANCE EDUCATORS

We have reviewed in this piece what is important to the financial institutions in the screening of prospective employees. The prospective employees are rising college graduates for business schools. We stress that all of the disciplines commented upon (above) are useful to the commercial bank regardless of the specialized views or biases of the educator. In our own experience we see far too many professors who happen to view their own specialized research strengths as exactly what the student needs to successfully land that first job. This is clearly wrong in that it is a disservice to the student. That student, we must remember, is the constituency of the first rank of the business school.

Lest it be lost in the discourse, we strongly put forth that the combination of finance training and accounting training is vastly superior to isolated training in either discipline. A closer intertwining of classwork between these two functional areas would benefit both the student and the financial institution. Casework, training in financial statement analysis, and personal computer applications can be coordinated more effectively with an eye to the student's marketability.

Enlightened business schools will want to directly discuss with major banking organizations in their region the specialized needs of this industry. The logic is the indisputable fact that finance departments like to place their graduates in the various fields of commercial banking. With this in mind, some active input from the banking industry on curriculum design makes good sense.

In the final analysis there is no substitute for individual responsibility. This extends to career choice and proper preparation for that career. Far too often, elected courses within university and college structured are wasted. We have tried to dwell on what the student can do now to enhance his or her opportunities in the financial institution arena. The last lesson is not to waste an elective.

This article was published prior to Barnett Bank merging with NationsBank.

Investment Banker

Reprinted with permission, The Princeton Review, Guide to Your Career.
Copyright 1996, 1997, 1998, Princeton Review Publishing, L.L.C.
www.review.com

A Day in the Life (Career Profile)

Investment bankers advise their clients on high-level issues of financial organization. They manage the issuance of bonds, recommend and execute strategies for taking over and merging with other companies, and handle selling a company's stock to the public. The work thus involves lots of financial analysis, and a strong background in finance and economics is a necessity. Personal and strategic skills are vital to investment bankers as well, for they serve as strategists for their clients, helping them develop their financial plans as well as implement them. At the profession's highest level, investment bankers serve as crucial figures in the shaping of the American and world economies, managing mergers of multibillion-dollar corporations and handling the privatization of government assets around the world. All this is time consuming, and investment bankers work long hours. Work weeks of seventy hours or more are common, and all-night sessions before deals close are the rule rather than the exception. Still, the work is extremely interesting, and those who stay in the profession report high levels of job satisfaction. Investment bankers spend large amounts of time traveling, to pitch ideas to prospective and current clients or to examine the facilities of companies being purchased by their clients. In the office, they spend their time developing strategies to pitch to clients, preparing financial analyses and documents, or working with the sales forces of their banks in selling the bonds and stocks which are created by the investment-banking department's activities.

Paying Your Dues (Major Employers)

In general, an M.B.A., requiring two years of post-college study, is required to rise in the field, though entry level jobs in analyst programs are available to college graduates who want experience in the profession. Analysts perform much of the grunt computer crunching required in preparing financial proposals, though they often travel to sit in on meetings with clients and sessions in which senior bankers pitch ideas to prospective customers. After two years, analysts usually move on, either to business school or to another profession, though a few are offered jobs as associates, the position which investment banks offer to M.B.A. holders. In many banks, this is as far as one can rise without an M.B.A., though there are exceptions, and a few prominent bankers never went to business school.

Associated Careers (Who You'll Work With)

Most commonly, investment bankers who leave the profession go on to financial jobs in-house with a client of their former banking firm, as financial officers and analysts. It is also not uncommon for bankers to move on to management consulting, a field which demands many similar skills. Some bankers get law degrees and become specialists in financial and corporate law, while lawyers sometimes leave their firms to become investment bankers. Bankers who have become sufficiently established, with clients who trust them and reputations for expertise in their fields, can become entrepreneurs, leaving their firms to set up their own investment banks.

PAST AND FUTURE (MAJOR ASSOCIATIONS)

Investment bankers have been around as long as stocks have been issued and bonds sold, but the current industry owes its form to the demand for expert counsel created by the increasing complexity of financial markets since the 1930s. Until relatively recently, investment banking was a fairly sedate field, but the 1980s saw tremendous growth in the field, as the increasing availability of complex securities and high-yield ("junk") bonds made mergers and acquisitions a weapon in the arsenal of every major corporation and made investment bankers like Henry Kravis and Robert Rubin extremely visible public figures. Though the stock markets have their ups and downs, companies always require expert advisors to help them sell stocks and bonds and to make strategic financial plans; investment bankers fill this need. Employment in the investment banking industry should remain strong over the foreseeable future.

QUALITY OF LIFE

Two Years Out: During the first two years after finishing business school and taking a job at a bank, most investment bankers work as junior associates, supervising the financial analysis done by analysts and themselves being closely supervised by more experienced bankers. At this level, associates are learning the business, acquiring the skills they will need when they are called on to develop financial plans rather than execute them. They spend long hours running computer analyses, preparing the financial reports which accompany stock issues, and putting together the documents used by senior bankers to pitch ideas.

Five Years Out: At this level, investment bankers have significantly more responsibility and mobility. They have become senior associates or vice presidents, depending on the structure of the firm, and oversee the preparation of documents that leave the firm, and they begin to be involved in the more creative side of the business, working with senior bankers and clients to develop financial strategies. They have established specialties, whether regional or by type of transaction, and have begun to develop the professional reputations and skills which will enable them to attract clients. Hours remain intense, and still involve all-night sessions and seventy-plus-hour weeks, but fifth-year bankers begin to have more control over their schedules. They have more control over their careers as well, as the options of going to work in-house for a client or moving to another bank with a specific need for their expertise become increasingly available.

Ten Years Out: By this point, investment bankers are involved in strategic and financial planning, creating the plans executed by junior bankers and spending significant amounts of time developing plans with existing clients and attempting to attract new ones. Those who have not left to start their own firms or to work for clients usually now have ownership interests in their firms, and they begin to participate in firm policy and management. They are responsible, either alone or with other senior bankers, for overseeing a sector of the firm's investment banking business, and professional success is now largely dependent upon the banker's ability to develop a client base. Hours remain long, but there is significant control over when work must be done, and pay increases dramatically.

CAREER PROFILE

# of people in profession:	40,000
% male:	90
% female:	10
average hours per week:	70
average starting salary:	$ 100,000
average salary after 5 years:	$ 300,000
average salary after 10 to 15 years:	$1,000,000

PROFESSIONALS READ:

Money Management, Wall Street Journal, Financial Executive, Institutional Investor

BOOKS, FILMS AND TV SHOWS FEATURING THE PROFESSION:

Wall Street, Sabrina, All That Glitters, Barbarians at the Gate

MAJOR EMPLOYERS:

Paine Webber
100 California Street
Suite 400
San Francisco, CA 94111
Tel: 415-954-6700
Fax: 415-954-5913
Contact: Linda Morris

Morgan Stanley & Co., Inc.
1585 Broadway
29th Floor
New York, NY 10036
Tel: 212-761-4000
Fax: 212-761-0086

Merrill Lynch & Co.
CIBG Recruiting
250 Vesey Street North Tower
New York, NY 10281
Tel: 212-449-1000
Contact: Human Resources

You'll Associate With:

Accountants, Financial Analysts, Researchers, Stockbrokers

Major Associations:

Institute of Financial Education
55 West Monroe
Suite 2800
Chicago, IL 60603
Tel: 312-364-0100
Fax: 312-364-0190
Contact: Lynn Murray

Association for Investment
Management & Research
P.O. Box 3668
Charlottesville, VA 22903
Tel: 804-977-6600
Fax: 804-980-9755
Contact: Human Resources

American Financial Services Association
919 18th Street, NW
Suite 300
Washington, DC 20006
Tel: 202-296-5544
Fax: 202-223-0321
Contact: Human Resources

Personal Trust Administration

M. Kathleen Hendricks
Vice President, Northern Trust Bank of Florida

TRAINING

Individuals come to Trust Administration from a variety of backgrounds. The most typical are banking and law.

Banking involves an up-through-the-ranks approach. A young person, fresh out of college and hired by a bank, is typically introduced to the various business units by employment in the support areas of those units. An individual's own interests and skills will usually dictate the areas where they will be most successful and advance. In addition to a college major in the areas of business or finance, the successful candidate for trust administration will be a flexible, detail-oriented, people-person who enjoys problem solving and a great deal of variety. In addition to on-the-job and in-house training programs, many state banking associations have trust school programs available to their members as part of a professional, continuing education program. There is an intensive, National Trust School/Graduate Trust School program offered through the American Bankers Association, as well as several privately run Institutes who offer programs for training administrators, portfolio managers, new business/marketing officers, and tax specialists.

Attorneys, who join the ranks of Trust Administrators, have generally had special training and often have practiced in the areas of tax, guardianship, real estate, probate, and estate planning. Because Trust Administration is essentially the management of a contractual relationship, attorneys are well suited to it with expertise in document interpretation and appreciation for the nature of the fiduciary relationship.

PERSONAL TRUST ADMINISTRATION

The administrators successfully manages fiduciary relationships. A fiduciary is a person having duty, created by his undertaking, to act primarily for another's benefit in matters connected with such undertaking. Although we think of the Trust as the foremost expression of this relationship, Agency and Custody relationships are also fiduciary in nature. Each relationship is defined by a contract; most of its terms are expressed in writing, but some are controlled by statute and common law. The Fiduciary relationships handled by banks concern *estates* (read: assets) as opposed to *persons*. The duties involved in the custody area are simply to safekeep the assets. Agency involves greater duties to manage assets that still belong to the principal. Trust includes the actual transfer of legal ownership to the trustee. In each situation, the Administrator must fully understand the relationship and assure that the fiduciary institution he/she represents is acting appropriately.

Fiduciary institutions employ a variety of specialists to handle the various needs of their relationships. In our particular institution, the initial, client-contact team includes the New Business Officer, Portfolio Manager, and Administrator. Once the relationship is up and running, the New Business Officer's involvement significantly diminishes, and depending upon the type of relationship and needs of the client, either the Administrator or the Portfolio Manager becomes the primary contact person. The Portfolio Manager handles the management of securities in the account; the Administrator handles everything else. Other resources available to the administrator include real estate managers, special assets (e.g., closely held corporations, limited partnerships, collectibles, minerals, etc.) division, tax analysts, legal staff, and the operations and support divisions. Many bank trust departments also have a division devoted exclusively to death-related situations and the estate-settlement process. Additionally the administrator works with the client's own attorney, accountant, insurance agent, and other professionals to assure consistency of direction.

HISTORY OF A RELATIONSHIP

The administrator's first contact with a customer is generally hosted by the new business officer and attended by the portfolio manager, customer, and one or more of the customer's family members and professional advisors. It is at this meeting that the players are introduced, the agreements (custody, agency, or trust) are signed, arrangements for the collection of assets are made, tax information is assembled, and the operational details (statement types and cycles, remittance amounts and methods) are worked out.

Once the assets are collected, a second meeting (except in custody relationships) is conducted by the portfolio manager, with the customer and administrator. The purpose of this meeting is to determine what the customer's financial objectives are and to tailor an investment strategy to those particular goals, mindful of the tax and market realities. Often a great deal of time is spent educating the customer in the basics of investing and the characteristics of various financial instruments. The more sophisticated the customer, the more efficient the process. Follow-up meetings are scheduled anywhere from quarterly to annually, depending upon the "personality" of the relationship, to review the progress of the portfolio and make any modifications dictated by changes in customer goals or circumstances.

Day-to-day activities are rarely predictable, and the servicing requirements of accounts vary according to type and customer need. A day's activities might include hiring household staff to assist an elderly or disabled customer, handling the gifting of securities on a customer's behalf, being proactive with tax planning suggestions, arranging for the payment of bills and fund transfers, and resolving operational problems. Since many customers seek our services because they are no longer capable of handling their affairs, we frequently make "house calls." Regular interaction with the customer places the administrator in the unique position of being able to alert other professionals to the customer's servicing needs and, in turn, enhances credibility in the professional community.

Death settlement is a specialized area of administration. The Administrative officer is often contacted by the family or attorney of the decedent customer shortly after the death and is often involved in making the necessary funeral arrangements and assuring that the burial instructions are appropriately carried out. Other duties might include, but are by no means limited to, meeting with the family and attorney, having the Will located and filed, locating and collecting any assets not currently held in trust, securing real estate, having personal and real property appraised, valuing all assets, preparing estate tax and income tax returns, paying all debts, administration costs, fees and taxes and distributing the assets in accordance with the decedent's wishes.

Administration of the irrevocable (unable to be changed or revoked) trust provides special challenges. Once the grantor is gone, the trustee assumes the responsibilities normally retained during his/her lifetime. The two most common types of "resulting" trusts (trusts created as a result of the death of the grantor) are the Marital and the Residual; there are variations of each, described by the ways in which they were funded, e.g., Credit Shelter Trust, Q-Tip Trust, and their purposes, e.g., GST Exempt Trust, Charitable Trust. Frequently these trusts call for distribution of all of the net income or a certain percentage of the market value to the beneficiaries on a regular basis. These trusts often call for the trustee to use his or her discretion in making payments from the trust assets, to the beneficiaries, according to a standard; common is, "as deemed necessary or advisable for health, comfort, maintenance and support." Frequently, the trustee is also directed to consider "all other sources of income available to the beneficiary" in making these decisions. Requests from beneficiaries range from college tuition and dental bills to fur coats and Caribbean vacations. Each presents a unique fact pattern and requires the trustee to consider a multitude of factors, in addition to the specific trust language, the size of the trust, the beneficiary's age and health, the interests of any other beneficiaries, the impact on the trust's ability to produce income, the tax impact of the sale of assets, and the "style to which the beneficiary has become accustomed," to name a few. Finally, the trustee is duty bound to also protect the interests of the remaindermen (those individuals or entities who will receive the trust assets upon termination).

Some other, common types of intervivos (created during the life of the grantor), irrevocable trusts include Charitable Remainder (Annuity and Uni-) Trusts, Grantor Retained (Income and Annuity) Trusts, Qualified Personal Residence Trusts, Rabbi Trusts, Life Insurance Trusts, and Florida's own "Flint" Trust, each with unique purposes, characteristics, and servicing requirements.

CAREER DEVELOPMENT, OPPORTUNITIES AND COMPENSATION

Many individuals who join the rank of Personal Trust Administrators make it a lifelong career commitment. As experience and skills grow, so do account load and account complexity. Because of the great variety of issues administrators deal with, boredom is not "job hazard"; it is possible to be challenged right up to retirement. Those interested in portfolio management, business development or management might find administration a useful experience, but not a prerequisite to success in those areas.

With the finance industry's growing appreciation of for fee-based sources of revenue, opportunities for employment in Personal Trust Administration have expanded significantly. While bank trust departments continue to grow, many brokerage houses, law firms and accounting firms have added Trust Management to their array of services.

Compensation varies significantly from institution to institution, geographically, and upon the duties the administrator is expected to perform, as well as experience. A career administrator can expect to earn a salary commensurate with those of other financial professionals with similar levels of responsibility. Many employers also have incentive programs that reward staff, including administrators, for generating new business.

CONCLUSION

Personal Trust Administration offers the rare opportunity to practice "financial social work," and to tailor, with sensitivity and expertise, solutions to meet the customer's needs throughout the life cycle of the relationship.

How to Use Section II

Caveats

Incomposing the text of the job descriptions, the primary emphasis has been to develop a consistent format that will convey information to the reader in a compact, straightforward fashion; hence, the outline format was selected. In order to preserve the authenticity of the survey-generated data, the words and phrasings that appear, are generally those provided by the respondents. In particular, several of the job descriptions give evidence of a "personal touch." This, of course, introduces perceptual biases, which may result in a job being described as the incumbent sees it rather than as it is or as it is seen by others.

The readers should be aware that no one job description can be considered representative of similar positions across all industries or all companies within an industry group. Because organizational structures often differ dramatically between seemingly identical companies, it's likely that the specific responsibilities and duties characteristic of a generically titled position—and the role or importance of that position within the overall corporate structure of the firm—will vary considerably from one company to the next.

Another bias of which the reader should be aware is that most of the information on specific job descriptions was collected from large multinational firms as listed in the *Fortune 500* and *Fortune 50* lists. The positions described, therefore, exist within the complex framework characteristic of some of the largest, most diversified organizations in the world. This introduces an element of job specialization, which may not be characteristic of typical positions in smaller organizations..

This book is written for the college student who has a basic familiarity with the discipline of finance. No attempt has been made to define such finance-specific terms as "ROI" or to explain what is meant by basic professional concepts such as "assess the financial markets."

Each job description is divided into nine subsections that present information pertaining to various components of the position being described. The nine subsections and the information they contain are:

Basic Function
The central theme or primary purpose of the position

Primary Duties and Responsibilities
Those tasks which are performed on a regular (and to some extent, repetitive or continuing) basis and serve, singly or in combination, to differentiate this position from other positions while providing a link to related positions which are either junior or senior to this position

Type of Decisions
The types of authority which have been delegated to this position, the extent to which they are exercised, and the extent to which reviews or concurrence must be obtained in order to take action

Consequences of Error

An assessment of the impact (on the firm or on the employee) of making errors in job performance

Organizational Relationships

A description of how this position fits into the hierarchies and lines of authority which formally exists in the firm's organizational structure

Work Relationships

The formal and informal contacts both inside and outside the firm which are characteristic of the position

Education and Experience

Depending on the source of the data, this may be a subjective (perceptual) estimate of the basic qualifications or a company-specific requirement for advancement to this position

Representative Skills and Knowledge

The specific skills and knowledge which are necessary (or perceived as necessary) in order to perform successfully in this position

Other

Usually a comment provided by an individual respondent, which offers some worthwhile or unique insight concerning the position

ACCOUNTING

Staff Assistant-Corporate Reporting

Basic Function: Assist in the monthly consolidation of the corporate books in order to prepare accurate and timely financial reports to management, the government and stockholders. Coordinate the timely and accurate preparation of all Securities and Exchange Commission financial filings.

PRIMARY RESPONSIBILITIES AND DUTIES
- Assist operating units in interpreting and implementing new accounting policies and concepts that are meaningful to local management
- Interpret financial reports
- Create new formats and reports to aid management's decision-making, and review current reports to see if they are still beneficial
- Advise division controllers of problems and solutions involved in booking new acquisitions
- Assist in the financial reporting of international subsidiaries
- Supervise the preparation of monthly balance sheet forecasting reports prepared for corporate treasury
- Maintain a current knowledge of accounting theories and practices as established by the American Institute of Certified Public Accountants and by the Securities and Exchange Commission
- Develop and implement new accounting practices at the corporate level
- Coordinate the timely and accurate preparation of financial data to be included in the annual report to stockholders
- Assist the manager of corporate reporting in managing and utilizing a major computer program for corporate data collection

TYPES OF DECISIONS
- Provide answers to questions raised by operating units based on corporate financial policies and generally accepted accounting practices
- Participate in decisions with the Manager Financial Reporting and the Director of Corporate Accounting as to financial matters on the corporate level
- Guide and make operating decisions for technically proficient accounting professionals
- Select and train subordinates
- Report results and unusual situations to immediate supervisor
- Plan and schedule work load and assign work

ORGANIZATIONAL RELATIONSHIPS
- The incumbent reports directly to the Manager of Corporate Reporting
- The incumbent must maintain a close relationship with the Law Department for continuous communication of financial information
- The incumbent reviews the performance of subordinates
- Either or both degrees should stress finance, accounting, and computers.

88

- BS degree in Accounting
- Should have three to five years in public accounting or three to five years in the general accounting areas of the company or its divisions

REPRESENTATIVE SKILLS AND KNOWLEDGE

Must have:
- A thorough understanding of accounting theory and practices (A CPA certificate, although not mandatory, is very desirable)
- The ability to communicate financial matters clearly to financial as well as non-financial management
- The ability to inspire employees to do a consistently accurate and timely job on all reports required

---

Staff Supervisor-Financial Reporting

Basic Function: To research, summarize, and represent the company on issues pertaining to authoritative accounting pronouncements and issues being studied by the Financial Accounting Standards Board.

PRIMARY RESPONSIBILITIES AND DUTIES
- Provide guidance during the preparation of summaries of authoritative accounting pronouncements and perform the first level of management review
- Supply management with information on current accounting issues
- Supervise the preparation of commentaries directed to the Financial Accounting Standards Board
- Represent the company's official position on debated issues and influence, if possible, the outcome of issues and enhance the company image
- Supervise the research and resolution of problem situations caused by the application of authoritative accounting standards
- Initiate projects internally or at the request of other departments in order to ensure consistent application of sound accounting theory
- Develop and present in-house technical training seminars in order to maintain the organization's quality of output
- Supervise the daily administrative functions of the unit

TYPES OF DECISIONS
- Prioritize assignments and establish target dates
- Determine the proper individual for an assignment based on project demands, time restraints, and professional development needs of the staff
- Select the most appropriate alternatives where diversified interpretations exist for an accounting issue
- Refer projects that involve upper management and/or would have a material impact upon the company's financial records, either directly or indirectly, to superiors

CONSEQUENCES OF ERROR

• The incorrect application or misinterpretation of an accounting issue could ultimately result in financial data being misstated. The total dollar costs of an error may vary from one project/issue to another but can be significant. If a material error were to occur, the company could be exposed to litigation from the public.

ORGANIZATIONAL RELATIONSHIPS

• Each project is unique thereby requiring instructions from a variety of superiors
• The incumbent provides superiors with formal input on subordinates' performance

WORK RELATIONSHIPS

• Formal weekly time reports and monthly status reports are prepared
• Formal and informal discussions occur several times a week
• Several personal contacts in other organizations are useful in providing valuable information
• The position allows visibility to and interaction with upper management

EDUCATION AND EXPERIENCE

• A BA in Accounting is required
• Experience with a public accounting firm and in internal corporate accounting/ auditing is valuable
• Continuing education beyond the BA is essential in order to stay abreast of current developments in both the accounting and management fields

REPRESENTATIVE SKILLS AND KNOWLEDGE

Must have:

• An in-depth knowledge of generally accepted accounting principles including a working knowledge of accounting research bulletins, Accounting Principles Board opinions, Financial Accounting Standards Board statements and technical bulletins, Accounting Standards Division statements of position, and various other authoritative literature
• Strong oral and written communication skills
• Strong leadership qualities
• The ability to manage time effectively
• Strong organizational skills

General Auditor

Basic Function: To perform audits in order to provide an independent and objective review; to assist in determining the direction and thrust of proposed audits; to analyze and appraise accounting, finances, and operations for assigned areas and activities of the company; and, to review, analyze, and appraise outside companies and organizations with whom the company conducts business.

PRIMARY RESPONSIBILITIES AND DUTIES

- Survey functions and activities in assigned areas to determine the nature of operations and the adequacy of the system of control to achieve established objectives
- Assist in determining the direction and thrust of the proposed audit effort
- Plan or assist in planning the theory and scope of the audit and prepare or assist in preparing an audit program
- Determine or assist in determining the audit procedures to be used
- Identify the key control points of the system
- Perform the audit in a professional manner and in accordance with the approved audit program
- Obtain, analyze and appraise evidentiary data in order to form objective opinions on the adequacy and effectiveness of the system and the efficiency of the performance of the activities being reviewed
- Make oral and written presentations to management during and at the conclusion of the audit to discuss deficiencies, recommend corrective action, and suggest improvements in operations and reductions in costs
- Prepare formal written reports that are expressed opinions on the adequacy and effectiveness of the system studied
- Appraise the adequacy of the corrective action taken to improve deficient conditions
- Discuss and explain audit findings and documentation with personnel from outside groups such as the independent auditor, the IRS, management consultant firms, etc.
- Be alert to real or apparent misconduct such as fraud, theft, embezzlement, etc. which may require strict confidentiality and sensitivity holding in the mind the company's best interest, auditing responsibilities and the auditor's code of ethics

TYPES OF DECISIONS

- The incumbent has considerable freedom to act on assigned projects within the constraints of division budgets, work schedule and policies, and general company policies
- The incumbent evaluates the adequacy and effectiveness of management controls and determines whether organizational units in the company are performing their planning, accounting, custodial, or control activities in a manner consistent with company objectives and high standards of administrative practices

CONSEQUENCE OF ERROR

- Error may result in loss of substantial dollar benefits in terms of improved operations, controls and procedures. In addition, error may lead to impairing the integrity of all company operations.

ORGANIZATIONAL RELATIONSHIPS

- The incumbent reports directly to the Director of Revenue and Inventory
- No positions report directly to the incumbent

- Specific auditing assignments may result in supervision of up to two support personnel

Work Relationships

- Audit activities may involve an office or field operations and personnel including six division offices, 44 warehouses and plant locations, six district offices, and 34 local sales offices
- Occasional trips may be taken to audit operations of various suppliers of services, materials and equipment
- Relationships with all company departments are at a management level high enough to discuss and reach agreements on audit findings of a confidential or controversial nature

Education and Experience

- BA required with emphasis or additional training in Business, Accounting, Finance, Management, or Engineering
- Experience and knowledge of the company's policies, organization, key personnel, operations, corporate systems, and formal and informal communication paths are necessary
- A minimum of six semester hours in computer science is required at this company

Representative Skills and Knowledge

Must be:

- Able to communicate effectively both orally and in writing
- Able to work effectively with people at all levels both within and outside the company
- Knowledgeable in EDP audit activities
- Able to understand accounting principles and control systems
- Able to accumulate pertinent data, organize material, develop and utilize sampling techniques, and make detailed analysis of existing conditions and appropriate recommendations

Other

- Because of the nature of audits, the incumbent must be fair and objective yet tactful in promoting constructive improvement or compliance with policy. This requires effective human relations, communications and performance. These must be combined with a proper humility and judgmental courage that at all times protects the company's best interest and builds attitudes of acceptance. The incumbent must be trustworthy and trusted.

Controller-Components and Materials Group

Basic Function: Formulate, coordinate, and maintain an integrated financial plan for the control of both domestic and foreign operations of the components and materials group. This includes responsibility for the proper accounting and control of $450 - $500 million of assets and $68 - $80 million of liabilities; measuring and reviewing the effectiveness of internal controls in all areas; maintaining control over all expenditures and the utilization and protection of all assets; reporting progress on short- and long-term plans; recommending action to improve or capitalize on current and long-range plans; and administering the C and M group budgets.

PRIMARY RESPONSIBILITIES AND DUTIES

- Advise the group vice president on financial matters, analyze financial results, and recommend action
- Formulate, implement and enforce accounting policies and practices that are consistent with corporate standards, legal requirements, and group and company directives
- Establish and maintain adequate internal controls to provide protection for all assets of the group
- Analyze projected market, business, environmental, and economic trends as to their impact on the short- and long-term financial requirements of the C and M group
- Assist in the formulation of a financial plan that will provide the proper return on an investment
- Develop, plan, and revise financial controls related to income statements and balance sheets to meet dynamic business conditions and group goals
- Recommend proposed investments in major fixed assets and substantiate the anticipated return on those proposed investments
- Develop and review the investment of domestic and foreign operations on an actual and forecast basis
- Develop tools for early identification of financial problems and make recommendations for resolution of the problems
- Review group operations and make recommendations to increasing profits through cost and expense reductions and income improvements
- Direct the group business systems activities in order to provide the group with the most modern, effective, and economical business systems operation
- Advise the group vice president in the area of foreign exchange and in the translation of foreign currencies
- Stay abreast of developments in the financial community and keep the group vice president advised of significant changes
- Provide cost and other financial information necessary to evaluate, review and analyze the C and M group's sales volume of $750 - $800 million
- Communicate methods and new techniques, law, taxes, etc. to the group Marketing Manager to assist in marketing decisions
- Review all sales and purchase proposals with unusual features or of large dollar value
- Serve as salary administrator for the C and M group
- Evaluate the necessity for legal, tax, community, and other areas of corporate resources to affect the proper solutions to business problems
- Select and assign personnel to maintain maximum utilization of knowledge and abilities

TYPES OF DECISIONS

- Analyze and recommend changes in financial reporting, financial analysis and financial policies
- Determine the best and most expeditious methods of preparing reports and analyses
- Exercise final review of limits of authority within the C and M group
- Interpret financial results, provide for remedial action, and forecast performance
- Review performance of subordinates, recommend wage or salary adjustments, and plan and schedule workload

ORGANIZATIONAL RELATIONSHIPS

- The incumbent directly supervises the Director of Business Systems
- Dotted line responsibility exists for 11 division controllers and 17 plant controllers/subsidiary controllers and for internal auditors
- The incumbent reports directly to Controller-Industry Products

WORK RELATIONSHIPS

- Coordinate and direct the consulting relationships between the controller's organization and other departments at the appropriate level
- Work with Marketing and Treasury personnel on special customer problems
- Serve as financial advisor to local colleges and/or civic associations

EDUCATION AND EXPERIENCE

- BS degree with a major in Accounting/Finance and an advanced degree in business required
- Should have one to two years experience in general accounting, one to two years in cost accounting, two to three years in financial planning, two to three years on the corporate staff, and three to four years as a division controller

REPRESENTATIVE SKILLS AND KNOWLEDGE

Must:

- Have a thorough knowledge of company accounting and financial planning procedures
- Be able to communicate effectively with top management in order to effect desired results
- Be able to administer many varied efforts and programs in all areas of operations
- Be able to plan, schedule, and execute overall operating responsibilities

Corporate Banking Officer

Basic Function: To maintain and expand existing relationships with clients by marketing all of the bank's services and to develop new client relationships.

PRIMARY RESPONSIBILITIES AND DUTIES
- Call on *Fortune 500* companies headquartered near the bank's offices
- Maintain existing clients in the face of product innovations, constant competition and the fact that many products have specified terms
- Identify opportunities for all of the services offered by the bank, including credit, cash management, pension management, foreign exchange, and interest rate exposure management, tax questions, and merger and acquisition activities
- Perform administrative follow-up on overdrawn deposit accounts, loan documents, rate information, memo writing for credit approvals, credit analysis, etc.
- Bring in the appropriate specialists to discuss technical products with clients
- Stay current with the technical aspects of new products
- Get to know customers better through personal calls
- Review files and annual reports

TYPES OF DECISIONS
- Overdraft approval
- Extension of credit to a client (including how much and at what pricing). Whether or not a specialist should be introduced
- Determining the best approach to take in convincing the bank's management that a deal is right
- Credit extensions require approval at higher levels
- Often the toughest decisions are about prioritizing activities

CONSEQUENCES OF ERROR
- A poor recommendation will either not get approved and make the person recommending it look foolish in front of superiors or be approved at the risk of losing significant funds/income for the bank and the department
- An unsuccessful recommendation of a good deal will result in a loss for my client
- The dollar amounts involved can be in the $100 millions
- What is said to a customer or superior can make or break a relationship (and a reputation)

ORGANIZATIONAL RELATIONSHIPS
- Informal discussions are held with the immediate supervisor at least monthly
- An annual review of performance is written and included in the personnel file
- Most work is performed as half a two-person team

WORK RELATIONSHIPS (CONTACTS)

- In-house communications take place with everyone from senior vice president to clerks
- External communications occur with chief financial officers, treasurers, assistant treasurers, and other financial officers

EDUCATION AND EXPERIENCE

- People with BAs are often successful as bankers as there is a good opportunity to learn the necessary skills on the job; however, it takes longer to develop skills that way
- The bank has an extensive six-month training program followed by regular seminars and "product knowledge" sessions while on the job

REPRESENTATIVE SKILLS AND KNOWLEDGE

- Be well versed in the bank's structure, function, capabilities, etc.
- Be knowledgeable of new products and people who have knowledge of them
- Know how to use the telephone, a calculator, dictating equipment, and a computer
- Understand present value analysis, international trade transactions, foreign exchange, swaps, and other finance techniques
- Be familiar with tax law, FASB rulings, and maintain a general familiarity with current market conditions
- Be able to use ratio analysis/financial analysis/credit analysis
- Be able to read and understand financial statements and footnotes
- Be able to digest information in a credit file to get a feel for relationship
- Understand the regulations governing lending limits relative to total exposure, reserve requirements, federal reserve bank effects on float times and documentation (as tedious as it is)

OTHER

- The job hours are of an 8:30 a.m. to 6 p.m. type with occasional late hours for specific jobs. Weekends are often used for review. This is a rare opportunity to see the working of many different kinds of companies.

Lending Officer-European Corporate Banking

Basic Function: Responsible for bridging the gap between U.S. subsidiaries of United Kingdom and Scandinavian-based multi-nationals and all of the services the bank offers.

PRIMARY RESPONSIBILITIES AND DUTIES

- Analyze credit worthiness of current and potential clients and projects submitted by clients
- Recommend loans or work with clients on "value-added" ideas in areas such as cash management, tax-related structures, leasing, money markets,

and mergers and acquisitions
- Develop strategies for covering specific accounts
- Advise senior officials within the bank of client needs or dissatisfaction

TYPES OF DECISIONS
- Credit decisions (primarily loan approvals) are made based on detailed financial analysis
- Lending decisions exceeding a specific lending authority must be referred to senior officers
- Innumerable decisions involving strategy for covering a particular account must be made

CONSEQUENCES OF ERROR
- The worst type of error would be a flow of funds problem; for instance, by placing a decimal point in the wrong place, a money transfer of $10 million may be authorized instead of $10,000
- Errors in analysis/decision-making have potentially negative effect on the job incumbent, other employees, the bank, and shareholders

ORGANIZATIONAL RELATIONSHIPS
- The European corporate banking division is broken down geographically by country
- The immediate supervisor is a unit head who in turn reports to a department head who in turn reports to the group executive responsible for Europe
- The incumbent directly supervises one secretary and provides limited input on trainees
- At least once a week (usually more frequently) the incumbent sits down with the supervisor to discuss the state of events with particular regard to clients. These usually take the form of critique sessions.

WORK RELATIONSHIPS
- Typically spend at least five hours on the telephone daily
- Have substantial personal contact both within the bank and with clients
- As many phone calls are initiated by the client, much work is of a reactive (putting out fires) nature rather than proactive type

EDUCATION AND EXPERIENCE
- A strong liberal arts background coupled with the bank's management program is sufficient

REPRESENTATIVE SKILLS AND KNOWLEDGE
Must:
- Have knowledge of generally accepted accounting principles
- Be familiar with legislation affecting banks and clients
- Read the trade literature regularly
- Know the organizational structure and the philosophy of the bank
- Have a good understanding of the political system of the countries in which you operate

In addition, should:
- Have strong oral and written communication skills
- Have strong analytical skills and enjoy working with numbers
- Be able to deal with people effectively
- Be a salesman and a diplomat
- Be able to prioritize work, i.e., have the ability to act on what is critical
- Understand the unwritten policies and philosophies of the bank concerning credit quality

OTHER
- The eternal questions become "Am I performing as well as I should, as well as my peers?" and "How well am I contributing to the continued profitability of the organization?"
- Honesty and integrity are extremely important

Marketing Officer

Basic Function: To provide a central focus for the metropolitan banking department's marketing program and to assist branch units in developing marketing strategies and plans.

PRIMARY RESPONSIBILITIES AND DUTIES
- Identify new and underdeveloped market opportunities for branch units
- Obtain and distribute solicitation resource material to branch units
- Monitor results of new business programs at branch units
- Coordinate new sales training programs for branch units
- Stay current with services/products provided by competitors
- Encourage discussion internally concerning the need for new and improved products/services
- Coordinate the development of new services/products internally with the Operating Department
- Develop and produce various promotional materials
- Develop and coordinate product knowledge seminars to keep staff members current
- Coordinate metropolitan marketing programs with other departments within the bank

TYPES OF DECISIONS
- Determine the priorities for numerous projects
- Design projects/products to meet specific goals
- Determine what course a specific project should take for implementation
- All significant projects (new products/services, training programs, etc.) that affect the staff, clients or other officers of the bank are reviewed with the immediate supervisor (the department head)

CONSEQUENCES OF ERROR
- Wrong information proved to staff members could embarrass the bank if

communicated to clients
- Depending on the magnitude of the error, significant business could be lost
- Products incorrectly described or not designed to meet the needs of a client can result in the loss of the client's confidence in the bank

ORGANIZATIONAL RELATIONSHIPS
- Supervise one marketing person and one secretary
- Maintain constant communication back and forth with the immediate supervisor (the department head)

WORK RELATIONSHIPS
- Constant contact with branch unit staff members
- Various degrees of contact with associates within the bank

EDUCATION AND EXPERIENCE
- An undergraduate degree is required
- The bank provides courses in communication skills, people skills, time management, knowledge of the bank, etc.

REPRESENTATIVE SKILLS AND KNOWLEDGE
Must have:
- Knowledge of the bank's operations, credit procedures, staff, policies, client base, and various jobs within the bank
- The ability to communicate effectively
- Strong interpersonal skills
- The ability to prioritize and effectively manage time
- A memory for details

Must be able to:
- Determine who within the bank will be most effective in solving a problem or assisting with a project
- Understand and stay current with the various laws and policies of government agencies such as the SEC and the FDIC

OTHER
- Must be creative, patient, and possess a sense of humor

Risk Manager-Financial Institution

Basic Function: To protect the company from adverse financial impacts of unexpected losses due to currency risk, equity risk, yield curve level risk, yield curve shape risk, basis risk, liquidity risk, counterparty risk, operation risk, and contract and/or legal risk.

PRIMARY RESPONSIBILITIES AND DUTIES
- Analyze market and other risks to which the firm is exposed

* Develop and recommend risk management strategies that focus on overall market risk and other risks faced by the firm rather than simply trading desk risk
* Determine the risks of particular markets faced by the various trading desks
* Aggregate the risk of all the desks to evaluate overall market risk faced by the firm
* Advise senior officials within the firm of risk management alternatives
* Monitor exposures and effectiveness of hedging strategies

TYPES OF DECISIONS
* Determine where risk exposures are greatest
* Work with senior management to determine which risks to hedge and the extent to which hedges will be constructed
* Select hedging instruments
* Structure monitoring programs

CONSEQUENCES OF ERROR
* Failure to account for inventory risk of spread trades and arbitrage, failure to correctly measure hedging risk, and failure to anticipate changes in risk can be catastrophic

ORGANIZATIONAL RELATIONSHIPS
* Position summaries from all trading desks required daily
* Review custom (OTC) contracts prior to signing
* Supervise staff of risk management analysts
* Report to CFO
* Staff support to Audit Committee

WORK RELATIONSHIPS
* Frequently meet with trading desk supervisors, legal department and information systems

EDUCATION AND EXPERIENCE
* CFA, MBA essential, Ph.D. helpful
* Strong math background required
* No substitute for experience (three-five years) in trading, environment and OTC contracting

REPRESENTATIVE SKILLS AND KNOWLEDGE
* Must understand complex pricing models
* Math skill, computer skills a must
* The ability to isolate risk factors of complex positions and aggregate factors into similar risk baskets is essential

Vice President-Credit Policy
(Financial Analysis Department)

Basic Function: To analyze and evaluate the credit-worthiness of one-of-a-kind projects submitted to the bank by various customers

PRIMARY RESPONSIBILITIES AND DUTIES
- Analyze credit exposure of the bank in the real estate and construction industries
- Write fee projects for bank customers
- Supervise and review the work of three other analysts
- Make presentations of finding within the bank and to customers
- Analyze, value, and rate (using the bank's own credit rating system, a system which has some parallels with the public agency rating system) the securities of various firms for customers of the bank

TYPES OF DECISIONS
- There is a constant stream of decision-making as problems faced in this department generally never have clear-cut answers
- Primary decisions are credit decisions and financial analytic decisions
- Personnel decisions occasionally have to be made concerning subordinates
- Credit evaluations are reviewed by the Rating Committee, the Credit Policy Committee, and others in the bank
- Fee projects are reviewed by an Internal Fee Project Review Committee
- Determining the manner in which information will be presented is almost as important as the information itself

CONSEQUENCES OF ERROR
- Errors can lead to incorrect credit decisions that can lead to substantial loan losses (minimum loss is usually $1 million)

ORGANIZATIONAL RELATIONSHIPS
- Credit review work is a requirement of the Credit Policy Committee of the bank
- All special accounts and credit with exposure over $3 million annually must be reviewed by the Financial Analysis Department Analyst
- Three subordinates report to this position
- Work is typically discussed with the supervisor once a week

WORK RELATIONSHIPS
- Infrequently meet with peers, bankers, and clients

EDUCATION AND EXPERIENCE
- A BA is required; an MBA is preferred
- All employees go through a training program for between three to nine months, depending upon prior educational and work experience and job destination

REPRESENTATIVE SKILLS AND KNOWLEDGE
Specific knowledge must include:
- Accounting
- Corporate Finance
- Macro-economics
- International Economics

- International Accounting
- Credit analysis and practice
- Public speaking
- Effective writing

In addition, the following skills are needed:
- The ability to analyze financial statements
- The ability to make industry comparisons
- The ability to assess risk
- The ability to effectively communicate results
- The ability to prioritize and organize work
- Fortitude
- A capacity to communicate effectively
- An ability and enthusiasm for working with financial statements

OTHER
- This position calls for a high degree of maturity and a capacity to maintain perspective in an intellectually chaotic environment

CONSULTANT-MANAGEMENT LEVEL

Consultant-Management Level

Basic Function: To analyze the clients of the firm in order to prepare an in-depth analysis for use as a blueprint to develop new business and to perform various contract analysis for clients, for example, merger analysis, and value management.

PRIMARY RESPONSIBILITIES AND DUTIES
- Analyze client needs
- Seek out new contracts
- Help clients solve various business problems
- Coordinate client and firm activities to accomplish clients' goals.
- Explore the business scene; make proposals to potential clients for using the firm and its expertise

TYPES OF DECISIONS
- Varies considerably depending on the client
- Most decisions concern what to recommend for clients

CONSEQUENCES OF ERROR
- Can be very costly
- Firm may be liable to suit should work fall below professional standards
- Position with firm is at stake

ORGANIZATIONAL RELATIONSHIPS
- All work performed is subject to review by the partners of the firm; the partner in charge of the department provides the final review
- Work progress is discussed with the supervisor on a daily basis
- The incumbent has the authority to direct and control activities of subordinates in analysis of clients' business organization and goals
- The incumbent does not handle grievances, hire or fire personnel but does prepare detailed work performance analysis for each subordinate; this analysis is transmitted to the personnel manager

WORK RELATIONSHIPS
- Frequently meet with people outside of the firm who are in banking, finance, and investment banking
- Meet with clients' personnel on daily basis
- Co-work with colleagues within the firm in systems analysis, internal control and computer systems analysis
- Participate in several community, business and charitable organizations

EDUCATION AND EXPERIENCE
- BA from a school of business administration from a recognized university

• Either of both degrees should stress finance, accounting, and computers

REPRESENTATIVE SKILLS AND KNOWLEDGE
Must be able to analyze:
- Financial statements
- Capital budgets
- Corporate organizational charts
- Systems of internal control
- Proposed mergers and acquisitions

Must also:
- Have a good understanding of corporate finance, cost of capital, capital budgeting, and various financial decision/analytical models
- Possess a good accounting background
- Possess the ability to work well with others
- Possess self-confidence, a high degree of intellectual capacity, and a desire to progress in your work at the expense of personal life
- Be able to assume responsibility
- Never stop the pursuit of knowledge

OTHER
- Services are usually rendered at clients' place of business. This job requires extremely long hours, frequent work on weekends. Severe time pressures exist with completion deadlines.

CORPORATE FINANCE

Junior Analyst-Finance, Planning, and Administration

Basic Function: Review the company's business plans and annual budget and analyze and summarize various financing proposals sent to the company.

PRIMARY RESPONSIBILITIES AND DUTIES
- Assess the financial markets
- Prepare a competitive analysis of the industry
- Prepare and review the corporate budget and business plan
- Provide financial research services and implement any decision taken in order to manage overall capital structure
- Gather, analyze, and summarize pertinent treasury information in report form
- Develop sinking fund strategy for repurchase of company bonds
- Implement borrowing decisions
- Participate in corporate and project financing
- Prepare specific management reports regarding financial performance as well as financial market performance
- Prepare for rating agency reviews
- Implement approved financial plans and policies
- Analyze, design, and implement a variety of computer-based information systems for worldwide treasury application

TYPES OF DECISIONS
- Determine company liquidity requirements
- Evaluate externally submitted proposals and determine whether they make economic sense for the company
- Determine whether requests from other locations meet specific guidelines of corporate policy

ORGANIZATIONAL RELATIONSHIPS
- Report directly to the Manager of Finance, Planning, and Administration

EDUCATION AND EXPERIENCE
- MBA

REPRESENTATIVE SKILLS AND KNOWLEDGE
Requires:
- In-depth knowledge of short and long-term financial markets
- Background in quantitative analytical techniques
- Knowledge of basic and advanced corporate finance principles, combined with mathematical and statistical analysis of finance alternatives
- Use of quantitative methods on the interactive computer

- Knowledge of computer-based approaches to managing debt information requirements
- Ability to participate on special study teams or task forces

OTHER
- Interpersonal skills and ability to communicate clearly are prime requisites

---

Financial Analyst-Revenue

Basic Function: Project future revenues for budgetary purposes and analyze past revenue performances.

PRIMARY RESPONSIBILITIES AND DUTIES
- Forecast company revenue for the annual budget
- Forecast company revenue for the rolling three month budget
- Provide an interface between controller and revenue accounting system
- Report company revenue in forms usable by other departments
- Provide a post analysis of last month's revenue performance and what caused deviations
- Respond to revenue questions raised by senior management

TYPES OF DECISIONS
- Choice of methodology
- Judging results of analysis as to the degree of reasonableness of any variance
- Superiors must review important methodology questions
- Superiors handle problems with data gathering

CONSEQUENCES OF ERROR
- If forecasts understate revenue to a large degree, serious cash flow problems can occur

ORGANIZATIONAL RELATIONSHIPS
- No subordinates
- Work progress is discussed with supervisor daily
- Revenue accounting is contacted for data

EDUCATION AND EXPERIENCE
- BA minimum; MBA preferred

REPRESENTATIVE SKILLS AND KNOWLEDGE
Must have:
- An understanding of variance calculations
- A knowledge of company and procedures on information gathering and presentation

- An understanding of company and industry structure and terminology
- Knowledge of company databases
- Presentation skills
- Writing skills
- The ability to use computers
- The ability to deal with others
- The ability to put things in their proper perspective

OTHER
- There is considerable stress associated with meeting deadlines in this position

---

Financial Analyst-Capital Budgets

Basic Function: Review capital and lease appropriation requests that require finance concurrence, coordinate and compile data for the annual capital budget, and compile actual and projected capital cash flows for reports.

PRIMARY RESPONSIBILITIES AND DUTIES
- Check accuracy of financial and accounting treatment of capital and lease requests
- Check for compliance with corporate regulations
- Prepare executive summaries for major capital projects
- Travel to obtain further details on capital projects
- Provide analysis and control prior to authorization of project
- Coordinate and compile data for the annual capital budget
- Analyze all projects submitted for the budget
- Prepare executive summaries on projected authorizations, expenditures, and variances from historical data
- Compile actual and projected capital cash flows for quarterly report

TYPES OF DECISIONS
- Interpret corporate regulations
- Prioritize projects
- Decide what additional information is required on an appropriation request before finance concurrence can be given

CONSEQUENCES OF ERROR
- The corporation as an entity is affected if appropriation requests with errors are authorized
- The corporation may allocate funds to inappropriate or unprofitable projects

ORGANIZATIONAL RELATIONSHIPS
- No subordinates
- Issues that have not been encountered previously are referred to higher authority

- If unable to reach agreement on an appropriation request, it is referred upward
- Have frequent contact with the manager and analysts in property accounting and the budgets manager of each division and each subsidiary
- Progress is discussed with supervisor daily

EDUCATION AND EXPERIENCE
- MBA
- In-house courses on computer usage

REPRESENTATIVE SKILLS AND KNOWLEDGE
Should have the ability to:
- Handle several projects of varying timing and importance
- Handle repeated critiquing and analysis of work
- Determine quickly the critical point of a project

Must have knowledge of:
- Reporting relationships
- Financial theory behind return on investment
- Corporate accounting procedures regarding capitalization, depreciation, equipment life
- Cost accounting (determining opportunity cost)

Additional skills:
- Be accomplished at mathematics, letter proofing, speed-reading, recall, diplomacy and tact
- Be able to motivate others
- Be able to clearly and precisely present ideas
- Have strong interpersonal skills
- Have stamina

OTHER
- This is not a routine job; it is very difficult to pre-plan activities
- Long hours are normal
- All direct training is on-the-job

Corporate Model Analyst

Basic Function: To analyze corporate models used in planning; to develop and maintain data gathering systems for systematic correct data input for model operation; to develop and maintain model systems which are consistent with corporate methods; to verify and analyze results of model output; to present and interpret model results to project initiators or to top management; and, to recommend subsequent action to project initiators and others.

PRIMARY RESPONSIBILITIES AND DUTIES
- Develop and maintain control systems for corporate model operations and

utilization including model validation, user priority scheduling, project records, and the training of support personnel
- Provide overall administration of division activities
- Design, program and test corporate model enhancements and modifications to reflect changes in company procedures and practices, tax laws, etc. and to provide for additional procedures to assist in the planning process
- Maintain detailed, up-to-date knowledge of corporate procedures and practices to insure that modeling procedures duplicate output of manual procedures
- Develop and maintain a base-planning forecast
- Review user requests in order to obtain a clear understanding of needs, special assumptions and conditions to correctly apply model
- Conduct analyses and studies (such as intermediate- and long-range budgets, forecasts, "what if" studies) for top management and other project initiators
- Analyze model results for consistency, meaningfulness, and correct application, interprets results to project initiator with oral or written presentations, and recommend subsequent additional studies or action
- Perform monthly outlook studies of corporate budget and analyze and interpret changes to the Budgeting Forecasting and Control Department
- Develop and administer user-training programs at all levels to encourage utilization of the corporate model
- Attend corporate model seminars and, through study, keep informed of continuing developments in the modeling field and evaluate if anyway they should be applied to the company's corporate model

TYPES OF DECISIONS
- Determine which programs are necessary to insure the continued existence of a modern, consistent and accurate corporate model
- Determine the necessary programs to provide a system that collects and controls data and corporate planning assumptions
- Determine procedures and provide necessary priority scheduling for division activities to meet divisional objectives
- Act independently with respect to assignments within the model area of responsibility
- Establish objectives and schedules to meet the needs of management and user departments

ORGANIZATIONAL RELATIONSHIPS
- The incumbent reports to Director of the Financial Analysis Department
- The incumbent supervises two Senior Corporate Model Analysts and one Model Analyst
- Annual planning interviews are set and reviewed quarterly
- Project status reports are reviewed monthly
- Appraisals are performed semi-annually to review progress, strong points, and weaknesses
- Immediate supervisor provides guidance of a broad policy nature

WORK RELATIONSHIPS
- Regularly attend department staff meetings

- Meet with company visitors to explain corporate modeling process and forecasting techniques
- Attend staff meetings of the Assistant Vice President in the absence of immediate supervisor
- Deal directly with various levels of management within the finance, controller, strategic planning and divisional departments as well as directors of general accounting, tax, finance, planning, etc.

REPRESENTATIVE SKILLS AND KNOWLEDGE

Must have knowledge of:
- Systems design and development
- Computers, programming and programming languages
- Management information systems
- Quantitative methods
- Financial analysis techniques and models
- Accounting practices and procedures

Must be able to:
- Relate to and communicate with people
- "Sell" services to others
- Understand a variety of business systems
- Format qualitative matter into a form acceptable to quantitative analysis and interpret results

---

Manager-Capital Budgeting

Basic Function: Responsible for budgeting and administering the company's capital asset expenditure program.

PRIMARY RESPONSIBILITIES AND DUTIES
- Compile and control the company's capital asset expenditures and construction program
- Analyze requests for capital appropriations
- Project future cash flow needs and analyze the resulting financing requirements
- Determine the amount and timing of future debt and equity needs
- Project and analyze financial statements
- Develop and maintain the computer system relating to capital asset analysis
- Prepare and present monthly reports on the capital expenditures program and cash flow projections
- Distribute information to and work with other corporate departments
- Supervise the identification of industrial revenue bond projects
- Supervise and review the calculation of various loan covenants and financial restrictions
- Obtain lease financing and assist in the issuance of industrial revenue bonds
- Negotiate terms of leases with lessors

TYPES OF DECISIONS
- Decide what methods will be used to control capital expenditures
- Develop the computer system necessary to provide relevant management information
- Negotiate the terms of lease financing
- Determine investment and use of industrial revenue bond proceeds
- Influence asset-user and financing departments to comply with capital budget constraints

CONSEQUENCES OF ERROR
- This position is very complex in that it concerns the entire company's operations rather than just one area; error may result in decisions to purchase assets with too low a return on investment resulting in an economic loss to the firm

ORGANIZATIONAL RELATIONSHIPS
- Direct supervision of Budget Analyst, Department Secretary, and Financial Analysts
- Decisions are reviewed by Vice President-Finance
- Present and exchange information with President, other senior management, division Vice President, and corporate department heads
- Work discussed with supervisor usually once a week
- Work with Legal Department for coordination of loan information and consultation concerning loan restrictions

WORKING RELATIONSHIPS
- Exchange of information with bond counsels and underwriters
- Provide directions on investment of bond proceeds to Vice Presidents of banks and leasing companies

EDUCATION AND EXPERIENCE
- MBA
- Three years experience in accounting or management accounting
- Three to four years experience in financial analysis and reporting with emphasis on capital expenditure decisions and cash flow analysis

REPRESENTATIVE SKILLS AND KNOWLEDGE
Must:
- Have analytical ability
- Be familiar with return on investment, internal rate of return, net present value, and other finance concepts
- Be resourceful
- Possess communication skills
- Have initiative
- Work well with people inside and outside the company
- Have an in-depth knowledge of financial analysis techniques and financial

computer models
- Be able to evaluate a variety of financial data and proposals
- Understand capital expenditure budgeting and control and cash flow analysis

OTHER
- There is considerable stress due to deadlines and conflicting priorities

---

Manager-Project Finance

Basic Function: Obtain financing as requested on facilities and on a project basis as appropriate to the corporate target capital structure and financial market conditions.

PRIMARY RESPONSIBILITIES AND DUTIES
- Assist with new corporate debt and equity issues and with refinancing to support the timely completion of projects
- Maintain a current knowledge of general corporate financing methods
- Work on special projects as required (such as research into various financing techniques)
- Put together and manage teams of investment bankers, lawyers, and accountants
- Analyze financings under management contract
- Initiate, negotiate, commit, and supervise other financing activities and projects

TYPES OF DECISIONS
- Select and evaluate the investment bankers, lawyers, trustees, and accountants needed to complete financing projects
- Select the financing vehicle appropriate to the project
- Determine the rates, terms, and conditions reasonable to the market and the project

ORGANIZATIONAL RELATIONSHIPS
- Represent the company at various external and internal meetings
- Responsible for the work of others including hiring, firing, coordination, review of work, and assignment of work
- Negotiate fees of consultants, investment bankers and lawyers
- Report to Vice President of Finance

WORK RELATIONSHIPS
- Work and interact regularly with:
- Lenders and underwriters
- Investor groups
- Industry groups
- Financial and industry publications
- Rating agencies

EDUCATION AND EXPERIENCE
- MBA with major in Accounting or Finance

- Five years experience in treasury/finance management positions with substantial experience in negotiation of financial transactions or investments

REPRESENTATIVE SKILLS AND KNOWLEDGE

Must have strong:
- Interpersonal skills
- Negotiation skills
- Analytical ability
- Problem solving/communication skills
- Originality/creativity
- Organizational skills

OTHER

- The heavy workload makes stamina a job requisite. It is necessary to project a positive image through personal appearance, knowledge, and demeanor

---

Manager of Financial Planning for Subsidiaries

Basic Function: Responsible for the financial planning functions, from a corporate policy point of view, for several subsidiaries of the company.

PRIMARY RESPONSIBILITIES AND DUTIES

- Evaluate external financing requirements of subsidiaries
- Prepare recommendations on financing for presentation to the Finance Committee of the Board of Directors
- Review financing plans and business plans of subsidiaries to ensure consistency with corporate financial targets
- Research and develop recommended corporate policy on a variety of financial issues, including lease vs. ownership of office buildings and hedging of foreign exchange transactions

CONSEQUENCES OF ERROR

- Errors could involve less-than-expected financial performance resulting in harm to shareowners

ORGANIZATIONAL RELATIONSHIPS

- The incumbent has no authority over subordinates
- Work progress is discussed with supervisor every day or two

WORK RELATIONSHIPS

- Frequently work with other individuals in related departments and peers in Treasury Department

TYPES OF DECISIONS

- Financial targets and policies are determined subject to review by upper management

EDUCATION AND EXPERIENCE
- Need MBA or BA in Finance with significant experience
- Various positions in treasury and accounting in company and its subsidiaries

REPRESENTATIVE SKILLS AND KNOWLEDGE
Must have in-depth knowledge of:
- General financial theory
- Cash flow analysis
- Cost of equity determination
- General accounting practices and procedures
- Understand the various functions performed by individuals in related departments (comptrollers, strategic planning, etc.)
- Have good writing ability
- Be able to see common financial approaches in seemingly unrelated areas
- Have the ability to work with others and the ability to learn

OTHER
- The position is characterized by frequent heavy workloads, short deadlines, and pressure to make correct financial decisions

---

Manager Financial Planning

Basic Functions: Accountable for the management of the Financial Planning Department with specific attention to the analysis, development and recommendation of system-wide financial goals including capital structure, return on investment and dividend policy.

PRIMARY RESPONSIBILITIES AND DUTIES
- Develop and recommend key financial goals and policies to executive management
- Direct the performance of tactical and strategic planning studies requested by management personnel and provide financial information and recommendations concerning possible financial alternatives
- Direct the preparation of financial forecasts, periodic updates and hypothetical studies in order to provide accurate forecasts, feasibility studies, analyses, and summaries of official financial forecasts
- Direct the preparation of financial impact analyses and recommendations concerning long-range facilities to determine the most economically desirable and feasible means of meeting energy and demand requirements, and communicate study results to executive management
- Monitor and define assumptions, data, and techniques used in developing financial projections, analyses, and recommendations and communicate these to management to further their understanding of the results
- Monitor and evaluate the impact of economic developments and forecasts and assist in the development of corporate strategy in order to establish goals and

objectives for the company and for use in future financial forecasts
- Direct the design, implementation, data management, user documentation, and ongoing validation of computerized financial planning models. Coordinate subsequent enhancement and usage in order to make use of technological efficiency and maintain as accurate and "state of the art" a model as possible
- Plan, develop, and implement the organization, personnel, and procedures necessary to provide various financial planning expertise and services
- Select, develop, motivate, and reward support personnel to ensure maintenance of an efficient and effective organization

TYPES OF DECISIONS
- Work priorities must be determined
- Personnel decisions are made
- Resource allocation among competing projects is a frequent problem
- Determine capital structure (debt/equity mix)
- Recommend dividend policy

CONSEQUENCES OF ERROR
- Could involve hundreds of millions of dollars which would affect stockholders, other investors, and the public (customers)

ORGANIZATIONAL RELATIONSHIPS
- The incumbent is responsible for 24 subordinates
- Discussions are held several times weekly regarding various work
- Formal reviews are held annually, but informal feedback on performance is given at least monthly

WORK RELATIONSHIPS
Frequently work with:
- Supervisory staff
- Other department managers
- Vice President of Finance

EDUCATION AND EXPERIENCE
- MBA required or BA in Accounting and Finance with 10-12 years experience
- Involvement in the management of the Corporate Finance area
- Work as a financial analyst in multiple Corporate Finance areas

REPRESENTATIVE SKILLS AND KNOWLEDGE
Must understand:
- Corporate and utility finance
- Capital structure and dividend policy
- General, utility and tax accounting
- Computer modeling
- System policies and procedures
- The interrelationships of companies in a holding company

- Electrical utility operations
- Public Utility Holding Company Act of 1935 and its applications to electric utility companies

Must possess:
- Verbal and written communication skills
- The ability to think clearly in a complex environment

OTHER
- This position has the typical pressures of middle management and time-related stress

---

Risk Manager-Manufacturing

Basic Function: To analyze the risk exposures of the firm and develop strategies to manage those exposures

PRIMARY RESPONSIBILITIES AND DUTIES
- Analyze the risks faced by the firm
- Seek out risk management tools available
- Develop and maintain risk control systems

TYPES OF DECISIONS
- Determine what risks should be managed
- From among the alternatives available, determine the best way to manage selected risk
- Determine procedures for monitoring risk exposures
- Establish benchmarks to meet the needs of management reporting

ORGANIZATIONAL RELATIONSHIPS
- The incumbent reports to the Chief Financial Officer
- The incumbent supervises the senior risk management staff and four risk analysts
- Risk audits are conducted annually and reviewed quarterly
- Immediate supervisor provides guidance of a broad policy nature

WORK RELATIONSHIPS
- Regularly attend department staff meetings
- Meet with senior management to explore risk exposures and report on the effectiveness of current risk management techniques
- Report to executive committee
- Deal directly with various levels of management within the finance, manufacturing, and strategic planning departments as well as directors of general accounting and tax

EDUCATION AND EXPERIENCE
- BA/MBA from a school of business administration from recognized university
- CFA helpful
- Education should stress finance, accounting and computers
- Financial engineering course work required

REPRESENTATIVE SKILLS AND KNOWLEDGE
Must have knowledge of:
- Commodities markets
- Currency markets
- OTC and exchange-traded risk management products (derivative contracts)
- Traditional insurance products
- Accounting practices and procedures relating to derivatives
- Financial analysis techniques and models
- Quantitative methods
- A variety of computer software

Must be able to:
- Relate to and communicate with people
- Understand a variety of business systems and risk exposures
- Format quantitative analysis and results into a form acceptable for qualitative presentations

---

Vice President of Finance

Basic Function: Plan, direct, and execute the long-term financing required to fund corporate capital requirements at the lowest cost

PRIMARY RESPONSIBILITIES AND DUTIES
- Plan and execute the financings required to fund corporate capital requirements while maintaining a balanced capital structure
- Direct, support, and review the actions of the department in obtaining long-term financing and maintaining positive relations with lenders and rating agencies
- Provide a capital budgeting and financial projection system
- Integrate projections of capital requirements with the status of credit markets and the company's capital structure
- Coordinate the activities of underwriters, lawyers, and accountants in order to complete financings in a timely manner
- Maintain contact with all company lenders and keep them informed of the company's goals and progress
- Provide financial support for various contractual arrangements
- Monitor pension fund assets and various special projects

TYPES OF DECISIONS
- Select underwriters, lenders, and counsel to structure financings
- Decide on the type of financing that is most appropriate to meet capital

requirements and financial structure targets at the lowest cost
- Determine the timing of the issue of new financings
- Decisions are reviewed by the Senior Vice President-Finance

ORGANIZATIONAL RELATIONSHIPS
- The incumbent directly supervises the AVP-Finance, Manager of Pension Investments, and Manager of Financial Analysis
- Work progress is discussed with the supervisor approximately once a year

WORK RELATIONSHIPS
Frequently work with:
- Bankers who are lenders and provide trustee services
- Long-term lenders (insurance companies)
- Investment bankers
- Investment advisors who manage pension funds
- Industry groups
- Legal counsel

EDUCATION AND EXPERIENCE
- MBA in finance or two to three years of progressively responsible experience in financial/investment analysis
- Five to six years (including at least three years of management) experience in investment banking, financial consulting, or a comparable job

REPRESENTATIVE SKILLS AND KNOWLEDGE
Should:
- Be resourceful
- Be a good communicator
- Have analytical/problem solving/creative abilities
- Have high degree of verbal, quantitative, and interpersonal skills
- Understand business principles and practices
- Have complete understanding of financial management
- Be a quick, clear thinker

OTHER
- This is a complex job with very high responsibility and visibility both inside and outside of the company. Feedback on success and failure is quick. Stamina is required for long hours and travel.

CORPORATE TAXES

Manager-Income Tax Compliance

Basic Function: Supervise the income tax compliance activities of the company and its subsidiaries in a way that will meet the statutory requirements of all taxing jurisdictions and protect the company's interest against excessive taxation. The primary responsibility is to control tax costs and compliance costs. This involves developing ways of saving and/or deterring taxes wherever possible.

PRIMARY RESPONSIBILITIES AND DUTIES
- Supervise the operation and filing of the consolidated federal income tax and all state and local income tax returns of the company and its affiliates
- Review all returns and make decisions concerning the treatment of all transactions included in the returns
- Establish challenging work performance standards for staff members and develop their professional competence through instruction
- Maintain a good working knowledge of the internal revenue code and related regulations, ruling, and cases as well as state income tax laws, etc.
- Analyze various transactions and procedures in order to develop ways of saving or deferring taxes and to reduce or eliminate compliance costs
- Coordinate the efforts of various group, division and subsidiary company controllers to assure proper administration of the income tax function
- Develop the information system necessary to assure proper and timely submission by subsidiaries and divisions of the financial data necessary for preparing tax returns
- Assist the company's independent accountants in their annual audits to assure proper settlement and make recommendations for appeals or possible litigation
- Assist in the preparation of responses to questions from the Internal Revenue Service

TYPES OF DECISIONS
- Determine who performs various work assignments
- Establish work priorities
- Select which information is to be filed with income tax returns
- Determine what information is required to assure proper preparation of income tax returns
- Approve employee requests for time off, vacation, etc.
- Subject to approval of the Director of the Tax Compliance and General Tax Council:
  1. Decide basis for preparation of income returns
  2. Select applicants to fill open positions within income tax compliance section
  3. Make salary and other recommendations resulting from the evaluation of the performance of subordinates

Organizational Relationships

- Directly supervise one supervisor, one senior tax accountant, four tax accountants, and one tax report typist
- Directly (or through subordinates) instruct and train headquarters and field personnel with respect to income tax requirements pertaining to the company's activities or policies and provide guidance for conforming to such requirements
- Report directly to the Director of Tax Compliance

Work Relationships

- Advise the Accounting Department as to the tax implications of accounting entries, procedures, and policies
- Examine the records of various businesses whose acquisition is contemplated to ascertain potential tax liabilities and recommended measure to minimize such liabilities
- Extensively read the tax literature in order to keep abreast of developments in income tax laws, court cases, and administrative interpretations, which may impact the company

Education and Experience

- BS or BA required
- A minimum of eight years experience either in the field of corporate taxation, public accounting, internal auditing or general accounting or any combination thereof is required

Representative Skills and Knowledge

- Must have a working knowledge and understanding of federal and state income tax laws, regulations, and court cases
- Must have the ability to analyze financial data from an income tax viewpoint
- Must have a complete understanding of basic accounting
- Must understand the company's financial and organizational structure
- Must be able to persuade other department personnel to cooperate with the Tax Department in matters relating to income tax compliance
- Must be able to motivate subordinates to work toward achievement of the same task

Other

- A high degree of administrative ability is required in directing the staff and organizing and planning functional work assigned.

Director-Tax Department

Basic Function: To manage the corporate tax function.

Primary Responsibilities and Duties

- Manage the preparation of the corporate federal income tax return and state

and local income tax returns
- Effect tax planning for the corporation's activities in the U.S. and internationally
- Make policy decisions on what position the corporation should adopt in respect to proposed business transactions, posture to be taken in respect of specific tax rules that would govern the reporting of income, deductions and credits
- Take positions in respect to federal and state legislative proposals, and present the corporation's views to committees of Congress and individuals and their staffs in the congressional bodies
- Represent the company in business negotiations, particularly those involving the acquisition and disposition of business enterprises
- Develop policy with respect to corporate tax litigation
- Represent the company to the Internal Revenue Service in the course of continuing audits

TYPES OF DECISIONS
- Apply corporate policy as it relates to tax matters and personnel matters affecting members of the Tax Department
- Determine what position should be taken in connection with corporate acquisitions or dispositions, major financing issues, legislative issues, and planning of international tax transactions

CONSEQUENCES OF ERROR
- Tax decisions often run into the 10's of millions of dollars
- Answers must be precise and correct because responses will be relied upon for decision making
- Credibility is particularly important

ORGANIZATIONAL RELATIONSHIPS
- The incumbent supervises 28 employees
- The incumbent has control over the 10-year promotion/salary increase
- The incumbent can hire and fire individuals subject to his supervisor's control over hiring new employees
- Discuss work with supervisor (the Chief Operating Officer) on an as-needed basis; probably occurs about twice a month

WORK RELATIONSHIPS
Have frequent contact with:
- Corporate Controller
- Corporate Treasurer
- Director of Industrial Relations
- Members of the corporate legal staff
- Senior executive management
- The tax staff
- Outside counsel

EDUCATION AND EXPERIENCE
- Minimum: BA in Accounting

- Most have a law degree, background in Accounting, and often a Master's degree in Tax Law
- Experience includes positions in tax compliance areas involving sales and payroll, state franchise and income, and federal income taxes
- Experience as a tax attorney in domestic and international tax planning is helpful

REPRESENTATIVE SKILLS AND KNOWLEDGE

- Must have knowledge of the Internal Revenue Code and regulations under the Code
- Must know the applicable decided case law affecting U.S. revenue rules
- Must be conversant with all state tax laws as they relate to corporations
- Must have good knowledge of foreign income tax, value added tax, and other transactional tax laws as they relate to corporations
- Should be skilled in managing individual employees and dealing with work related problems
- Should be able to present ideas verbally and in writing with precision and clarity to lay people not familiar with tax laws or accounting principles
- Must be able to present ideas with precision, both in writing and verbally, to individuals who are highly conversant and skilled in the technical tax area
- Must have imagination
- Should be skilled in interpreting highly complex rules

```
┌─────────────────────────────────────────────┐
│                  INSURANCE                    │
└─────────────────────────────────────────────┘
```

Director of Risk Management

Basic Function: To protect the company from the adverse financial impact of significant unexpected losses using self-insurance, captive insurance, loss control methods, safety techniques, and conventional or non-conventional insurance; and, to provide guidance and assistance to other staff and operating units concerning risk management, insurance, or claim situations.

PRIMARY RESPONSIBILITIES AND DUTIES
- Plan and establish long-range risk management objectives
- Identify the corporate exposures to loss and the measurement of these risks in terms of their frequency, severity and financial impact
- Develop, implement and maintain an overall risk management program that utilizes the most effective and economical balance of self-insurance, loss-control methods, insurance, and related services
- Design, analyze, negotiate and purchase the appropriate insurance coverages, select brokers and supervise contract services provided by consultants, brokers and insurance agents
- Maintain effective communication with other departments, divisions and subsidiaries, providing assistance in the administration of risk management programs and in obtaining data
- Assist in the implementation of safety/property conservation programs; recommend other loss control procedures
- Research, plan and control all self-insurance programs and establish corporate policy as to risk retention or insurance
- Monitor all insurance methods and procedures within the corporation
- Review the effects of mergers, acquisitions, divestitures, and join ventures from a risk management point
- Complete special projects as assigned

ORGANIZATIONAL RELATIONSHIPS
- The incumbent reports to the Deputy Treasurer
- No supervision assigned

WORK RELATIONSHIPS
Frequent interaction is required with:
- Operating companies' CEO or Vice President-Finance or Controller; all corporate staff positions, especially those involved in finance or law; and risk managers from other large corporations
- Executives of large insurance brokerage organizations
- Government officials
- Insurance company executives
- Underwriters, claims attorneys, or joint venture partners

- Personnel of the New York Insurance Exchange
- Various professional organizations

EDUCATION AND EXPERIENCE

- BS degree with a minimum of eight years experience
- Executive hands-on experience managing an insurance company is mandatory
- MBA coursework and AMA and RIMS seminars are all valuable

REPRESENTATIVE SKILLS AND KNOWLEDGE

Must understand:

- Commission insurance brokerage operations
- Worldwide insurance markets
- Underwriting practices
- Claims procedures
- Legal technicalities
- The actuarial sciences
- Accounting
- Insurance policy wording

INVESTMENTS

Securities Analyst-Common Stock

Basic Function: Prepare company and industry-wide analyses of common stocks, interview outside-corporation management, summarize, and interpret information, and recommend appropriate action by a presentation to the investment committee.

PRIMARY RESPONSIBILITIES AND DUTIES
- Analyze companies and industries to determine suitability for common stock investments; determine prospects for future growth and assist in maintenance of portfolio
- Review common stock presently in the portfolio to assure continued acceptability to company objectives
- Consider and evaluate alternative investment scenarios
- Gather necessary information from divisional records, outside sources, and financial reports
- Compile information into summaries with recommendations and make presentations to senior officers and to the investment committee
- Prepare statistics relating to common stock or equivalent investments
- Participate in investment process by mastering and improving upon traditional analytical approaches

TYPES OF DECISIONS
- Determine the suitability of present or prospective investments based on company objectives
- Establish priorities for individual research
- Aggressively discover and pursue investment ideas in an expeditious manner
- Determine the value of alternative investment possibilities

ORGANIZATIONAL RELATIONSHIPS
- The incumbent reports to the Investment Officer
- Contact corporate management of outside firms

EDUCATION AND EXPERIENCE
- Required to have a two to three years' experience
- MBA is desirable

REPRESENTATIVE SKILLS AND KNOWLEDGE
Must:
- Possess human relations skills, tact, and diplomacy
- Have excellent skills in preparing oral and written reports
- Have a high degree of judgment
- Be able to develop ideas in a concise and meaningful conceptual framework
- Show initiative

Additionally:
- A comprehensive knowledge of investment analysis, economic principles, company and industry trends, market judgment, and sense of market timing
- A knowledge of company policies, practices, and objectives

Securities Analyst-Private Placements

Basic Function: To manage two to five industrial categories of the firm's fixed-income portfolio.

PRIMARY RESPONSIBILITIES AND DUTIES
- Collect, organize, and analyze industry and company data to determine the relative attractiveness of various investments
- Make presentations to three layers of internal senior management
- Responsible for negotiation and documentation of loans, as well as amendments and waivers on such loans
- Supervise payout of loans
- Work with the commercial mortgage department on credit deals involving mortgages
- Occasionally work on equity investments in assigned industries
- Responsible for managing company's fixed-income investments
- Meet with top management of the borrowing company
- Conduct general industry research
- Service amendments to existing loans
- Negotiate loan's legal terms and definitions
- Determine the competence of outside management and overall creditworthiness of borrower

CONSEQUENCES OF ERROR
- If there is an error in the analysis of the borrowing company and they default, the loss could be 100% ($1 million to $30 million)
- The company's customers (life insurance and pension recipients) would ultimately bear any costs

ORGANIZATIONAL RELATIONSHIPS
- No subordinates
- Work progress is discussed with the supervisor (Senior Investment Manager) every couple of days
- All decisions by analyst are referred up the management chain, usually several levels
- There is frequent contact with the Vice President-Fixed Income Securities, the Senior Vice President, the Bond Committee, the Finance Committee, the Associate Counsel, and the Associate Secretary-Securities

WORK RELATIONSHIPS
Frequently work with:
- Investment bankers who call with potential investments

- Outside special counsel
- Lawyers to approve final negotiated terms of loan agreements
- Securities Analyst - Private Placements
- Borrowers

EDUCATION AND EXPERIENCE

- MBA
- Should be educated in investments, economics, accounting, finance, English and math
- Informal on-the-job training is provided

REPRESENTATIVE SKILLS AND KNOWLEDGE

Should understand:
- Principles of investment finance such as present value, compound interest and pricing of bonds

Should have:
- The ability to use pre-written computer programs
- The ability to write programs
- Good speaking skills
- Self-assurance
- Negotiating skills
- The ability to work in a totally unstructured environment
- Analytical skills
- Business judgment skills

OTHER

- There are numerous deadlines that frequently cause stress.

Direct Loan Analyst

Basic Function: To assess the financial condition and performance of existing and potential borrowers; to analyze direct loan offerings made to the company to determine the acceptability of the offerings to company standards; to prepare recommendations on such offerings; to participate in negotiations and review loan agreements; and to monitor the stability of firms receiving loans.

PRIMARY RESPONSIBILITIES AND DUTIES

- Interview and evaluate outside corporate management to obtain facts to judge and estimate future performance
- Paint a quantitative picture of a company's financial health (profitability, cash flow, leverage, etc.)
- Evaluate the stability and future financial expectations of offering firms
- Numerically assess the expected return on potential investments
- Maintain contact with assigned investment bankers to obtain a flow of

acceptable offerings
- Review common stock warrant holdings in connection with loan agreements
- Review requests to modify existing agreements
- Analyze requests for modification of existing direct placement loan agreements
- Assist in problem loan workouts by analyzing company's financial situation
- Assist in training lower-level staff
- Develop new business

TYPES OF DECISIONS
- Recommend action on direct loan submissions
- Recommend action on requests for modification of loan agreements
- No decisions are actually made other than basic data and analysis decisions

ORGANIZATIONAL RELATIONSHIPS
- The incumbent reports to various investment officers

WORK RELATIONSHIPS
- Frequent contact with the finance committee, outside management, investment bankers, and lawyers

EDUCATION AND EXPERIENCE
- MBA
- 2 1/2 years experience in securities analysis

REPRESENTATIVE SKILLS AND KNOWLEDGE
- Accounting practices (revenue recognition, various methods for valuing balance sheet accounts, and procedures to assess the quality of reported earnings)
- Financial statement analysis (understand measures of profitability, operating efficiency, leverage, and asset quality to determine a company's financial health)
- Discounted cash flow analysis (understand time value of money, dissect a proposed transaction, and determine the magnitude and timing of cash flows)
- Basic investment and economic principles
- Have the ability to work independently
- Possess good mathematical ability
- Have good human relations skills and be able to communicate orally and in writing

OTHER
- This position can cause stress for analysts as they must constantly re-determine what the investment goals and prospects are at any particular time.

Securities Analyst-Publicly Traded Bonds

Basic Function: Analyze publicly traded industrial and utility bonds to determine their acceptability to company standards, prepare recommendations regarding such offerings, and monitor the condition of the firms whose bonds are purchased.

Primary Responsibilities and Duties
- Review the company's portfolio on an on-going basis to assure continued acceptability to company standards
- Recommend sales or additional purchases
- Analyze bids received for the purchase of public bonds, determine impact, and recommend course of action
- Evaluate corporate management, compile information obtained, and prepare and submit recommendation to senior investment officers
- Prepare periodic reports on the status of the bond portfolio for the finance committee
- Act as a back-up for investment/research activities

Types of Decisions
- Determine quality of corporate management and financial standings of companies offering bonds
- Recommend purchase or sale of public bonds in response to unanticipated changes in public offerings
- Identify specific problems with the public bond portfolio and recommend appropriate course of action
- Evaluate market and industry trends and recommend purchase/sale strategies

Consequences of Error
- Errors in analysis or judgment can result in financial loss or lost investment opportunities

Organizational Relationships
- The incumbent reports to the Senior Investment Officer

Work Relationships
Occasionally work with:
- Outside managements
- Brokers

Education and Experience
- At the first level, a college degree with some business courses in accounting, finance and/or economics; some prior experience in a financial environment
- At the middle level, approximately two years directly related experience
- At the top level, approximately four years directly related experience; an MBA desirable

Representative Skills and Knowledge
- A knowledge of finance, investments, accounting and economics
- A knowledge of company policies and practices regarding the public bond market
- Continually increase knowledge of the public industrial and utility bond market
- Have strong analytical skills, good judgment and good oral and written communication skills
- Be good at human relations

Portfolio Analyst

Basic Function: Perform administrative and information-gathering functions in connection with the company securities division and the company's securities portfolio.

PRIMARY RESPONSIBILITIES AND DUTIES
- Prepare various company and industry reports, both weekly and monthly, for use internally
- Review reports by other divisions
- Determine qualifications of securities investments
- Prepare and file necessary paperwork on loans
- Monitor delinquent loans
- Prepare annual and semi-annual reports for the finance committee
- Analyze financial statements received on portfolio credits
- Assist in the maintenance of the company portfolio by recommending specific actions

TYPES OF DECISIONS
- Determine logical frameworks and mathematical approaches to analyzing and presenting data and recommend changes in format
- Recommend and implement new procedures and controls for information processing
- Make recommendations and take appropriate action based on various reports

CONSEQUENCES OF ERROR
- Erroneous information in reports could adversely affect creditability of internal policies and effectiveness of external policies
- Failure to follow up on delinquent or late payments could result in deterioration of company's lending position
- Errors in analysis and judgment could result in loss of security or reduced realization upon liquidation of a borrower

EDUCATION AND EXPERIENCE
- MBA
- Two to three years experience in securities analysis

REPRESENTATIVE SKILLS AND KNOWLEDGE
- Possess human relations skills to effectively negotiate
- Have judgment and analytical skills
- Have the ability to analyze company's financial reports
- Have a solid background in finance, economics, and/or accounting

---

Manager-Pension Fund Investments

Basic Function: Responsible for the prudent management of the assets held by the employees' pension fund, the control of appropriate administration expenses (trustee and consultant fees, brokerage commissions, etc.), the allocation of assets among investment managers, and the diversification of assets by type of security.

PRIMARY RESPONSIBILITIES AND DUTIES
- Determine the specific breakdown of pension fund investments among asset types based on analysis aimed at maximizing returns while maintaining liquidity
- Select, supervise, and evaluate the investment managers and negotiate compensation
- Select and supervise outside investment managers for the pension fund
- Analyze large general corporate financing proposals and recommend best financing "deals"
- Obtain stock for the employees' stock bonus plans through open market purchase or the new issue market
- Recommend and implement amendments and revisions to trust, investment manager, and consultant agreements
- Develop measurements and evaluation reports for monitoring the performance of investment managers
- Study, evaluate, and recommend new investment opportunities, techniques, and practices
- Conduct quarterly investment review meetings with investment managers
- Report quarterly to the Pension Plan Administration Committee and annually to the Audit Committee of the Board of Directors on the investment management of the pension funds
- Represent the corporation at seminars and conferences to maintain a high level of awareness of new developments and changes in pension fund management and pension legislation
- Undertake special assignments as requested by the Vice President-Pension Investments and Investor Relations

TYPES OF DECISIONS
- Decide the appropriate mix of investments considering current and projected market conditions
- Select or dismiss investment managers, trustees, and consultants
- Set investment objectives and policies
- Determine criteria for measuring the performance of managers

CONSEQUENCES OF ERROR
- The quality of decisions on investment types and managers has substantial financial impact on the cost of funding employee benefits and the safety of the principle of the fund's assets

ORGANIZATIONAL RELATIONSHIPS
- The incumbent supervises investment managers, the Vice President of Performance Analysis, one pension fund analyst, and one senior investment clerk
- Work progress is discussed frequently with the incumbent's supervisor
- Decisions are usually reviewed by the Vice President of Finance

WORK RELATIONSHIPS

- Must oversee performance of various bank trust officers
- Work frequently with Vice Presidents and/or Presidents of investment management companies and banks
- Work frequently with research Vice Presidents and/or investment banking economists
- Speak or serve as discussion leader at various pension seminars and conferences
- Serve as an advisor on pension plan management to institutions such as universities, hospitals, endowment funds and charitable organizations
- Maintain contacts and relationships with outside sources of information such as the investment community, trade publications, peer groups, conferences, and seminars

EDUCATION AND EXPERIENCE

- MBA in Finance and/or Chartered Financial Analyst designation
- Three to five years in investment analysis or portfolio management

REPRESENTATIVE SKILLS AND KNOWLEDGE

- Understand corporate financing methods
- Be conversant with the Internal Revenue Code
- Be conversant with the Employment Retirement Income Security Act of 1974
- Understand fundamental business principles and practices
- Understand the Federal Reserve Board's monetary policy
- Possess good analytical ability
- Have strong communication skills
- Have strong verbal, quantitative, and interpersonal skills
- Be able to organize and plan workloads
- Be able to prioritize
- Have an in-depth knowledge of government fiscal policy, math, statistical analysis, accounting, and economics

OTHER

- This position requires that the incumbent be able to successfully articulate new ideas and concepts, persuade and motivate investment managers, negotiate and bargain fees and services, and, most importantly, persuade others to act.

Director-Investor Relations

Basic Function: Primary work is in investor relations with additional responsibility for pension fund investments and corporate financings.

PRIMARY RESPONSIBILITIES AND DUTIES

- Keep informed on business conditions of all company operating subsidiaries, strategic planning directions, and financial developments at the corporate level

- Stay abreast of industry matters to help explain external influences on the company as well as to keep up with the operating and financial results of the company and its competitors
- Communicate on a daily basis with the investment community in order to accurately portray company results and general expectations within the guidelines of SEC policy
- Arrange meeting times and places for senior management presentations around the country with investment analyst groups
- Act as host to analysts who visit company
- Establish plans and procedures when company hosts inspection trips or special seminars requiring special coordination among operating subsidiaries
- Select and set up personal meetings with institutional owners in order to develop greater support for our stock by the institution's portfolio managers
- Prepare monthly reports on investor relations matters, review policy and plans, and make recommendations for changes
- Monitor investment results of six investment managers
- Prepare monthly and quarterly reports on results and outlook
- Work with actuary and consultants on long-term strategy, including asset allocation and manager selection

ORGANIZATIONAL RELATIONSHIPS
- The incumbent reports to the Deputy Treasurer
- Frequent contacts include Senior Vice President and Chief Financial Officer, personnel in finance and other departments, subsidiary Presidents/Vice Presidents and outside directors/managers
- No supervision assigned

EDUCATION AND EXPERIENCE
- MBA
- Pension fund educational seminars
- Five to ten years in industry and/or association businesses

REPRESENTATIVE SKILLS AND KNOWLEDGE
- Understand and communicate the impact of various external factors (Federal Reserve policy, fiscal policy, competition, etc.) on the company's financial health
- "Sell" the company and its performance to others
- Plan, prioritize, and allocate time among many competing tasks
- Use a calculator and several financial modeling/analytical techniques
- Understand and interpret various accounting statements

OTHER
- This position entails a standard workday and week with about 20% overtime.

Account Executive (Securities Broker)

Basic Function: Provide advice and counsel to clients concerning potential investments; execute purchase, sell, and other trade orders on behalf of clients.

PRIMARY RESPONSIBILITIES AND DUTIES
- Make investment recommendations to clients
- Execute trades on behalf of clients
- Expand market through new contacts and clients
- Learn new investment products
- Serve as a liaison between bookkeeping and clients
- Review research to stay current with several markets

CONSEQUENCES OF ERROR
- Clients can lose money
- The broker can lose a source of income

ORGANIZATIONAL RELATIONSHIPS
- Performance is formally reviewed on a quarterly basis
- Market conditions are appraised and discussed continuously with analysts and others
- The incumbent has authority over one sales assistant

EDUCATION AND EXPERIENCE
- BA in Finance
- Four-month company training program
- Must pass a six-hour exam to register as a securities representative with the New York Stock Exchange
- Must be licensed in such states as you give investment advice in (usually requires a two-hour exam)

REPRESENTATIVE SKILLS AND KNOWLEDGE
Must have:
- The ability to assimilate massive quantities of information
- The ability to communicate clearly and directly with others
- Should be capable of time and stress management

Must understand:
- The mechanics and strategies of American securities trading and the SEC acts of 1933 and 1934
- SEC rules 144, 147, 146, 237; Regulations A, G, Q, T, and U
- Prudent Man Rule
- NYSE 405
- NASD Codes of Arbitration and Procedure
- Rules of fair practice

In addition:
- Must be able to get people to define their financial objectives clearly and concisely
- Must not be afraid of failure

OTHER
- There is great uncertainty in terms of products, markets, and salary. In addition, there is continual pressure from management to expand product expertise and market penetration.

Mortgage Analyst-Production

Basic Function: To handle all matters related to the production, analysis, and negotiation of applications for the acquisition of conventional mortgage loans and real estate investments.

PRIMARY RESPONSIBILITIES AND DUTIES
- Negotiate terms, conditions, interest rates, etc. to obtain a flow of acceptable applications for conventional loans and opportunities to purchase real estate
- Analyze client's financial status and past performance, type of property, nature of offer, property location, facilities and access, and competition
- Inspect property under consideration
- Prepare detailed analyses of proposed loan or purchase and recommend action on offerings
- Prepare mortgage committee memoranda in conjunction with supervisor and present recommendations to the officer in charge of the mortgage committee
- Prepare commitment letters on those investments that have been approved by the committee
- Assist in the negotiation of the final commitment terms and conditions
- Work with client to help resolve problems which may jeopardize company's rights under a mortgage
- Prepare correspondence under own signature or for signature by supervisor on all aspect of application processing

TYPES OF DECISIONS
- Must determine pertinent details necessary for proper analysis of loan/purchase offers
- Responsible for negotiating terms, conditions, interest rates, etc.
- Make accept/reject recommendations to supervisor and the mortgage committee

CONSEQUENCES OF ERROR
- Negotiations conducted to the best advantage of the company will result in the acquisition of high-yield investment opportunities and the addition of sound investments to the mortgage and real estate portfolio; error will result in low yield properties and/or unsound decisions

ORGANIZATIONAL RELATIONSHIPS
- This is one of three non-officer mortgage analyst positions that can be differentiated by the amount of experience required, the complexity of the duties performed, and the degree of independence with which the duties are performed

WORK RELATIONSHIPS
- Work regularly with developers, brokers, services, and mortgage bankers
- Recommend actions to senior mortgage officer
- Reports are made to the officer in charge and to the mortgage committee
- Work is done with the staff of the administrative and closing units of the divisions of investment Law and Accounting regarding closings and modifications
- Work is performed within the confines of management specifications, legal requirements, and within the scope of authority granted

EDUCATION AND EXPERIENCE
- No specific educational requirements
- Two to three years in mortgage analysis required

REPRESENTATIVE SKILLS AND KNOWLEDGE
Requires:
- A knowledge of economics, business, mortgage banking, and real estate
- A command of accounting principles and practices

Must:
- Have sound analytical abilities in order to judge the acceptability of offerings
- Be a strong negotiator
- Be able to appraise the potential of a given investment where past performance criteria are not available
- Know legal requirements and restrictions affecting acquisition of investment properties

OTHER
- The ability to be tactful and discreet is essential, especially when informing a developer with whom future dealings are desired that a particular transaction must be declined. Strong human relations skills are essential.

Mortgage Analyst-Closing

Basic Function: To coordinate all business matters, relating to the closing of conventional mortgage loans and real estate; to analyze requests for, negotiate, and recommend changes in commitment terms.

PRIMARY RESPONSIBILITIES AND DUTIES
- Responsible for coordinating all loan closing details on mortgage loan commitments on a timely basis
- Obtain required closing documents such as operating agreements, title reports, leases, appraisals, plans, and specifications
- Analyze closing documents and related exhibits to insure that details are in agreement with the original commitment terms

- Submit plans, specifications, and appraisals to appraisal and engineering staff for review and approval
- Consult with the real estate production section on interpretation of requirements set forth in original commitment letters where discrepancies or problems appear to exist
- Reconcile discrepancies/problems with clients
- Evaluate requests for changes in, or variances from, commitment terms including requests for modification, loan increases, lease substitutions, substitution of liability, etc.
- Analyze requestors' financial status, type of property, location, past performance, etc. to determine if proposed modifications to commitment terms make good business sense and the nature of their impact on the company's financial position
- Ascertain whether a particular business decision is compatible with legal requirements
- Inspect exterior and interior of properties prior to all loan closings to insure that all physical requirements (facilities, access, etc.) adhere to the original commitment terms of proposal and determine the effect certain requested changes will have on the property
- Prepare written reports on finding to appraisal/engineering staff recommending further investigation
- Negotiate changes in conditions and closing details with clients
- Draft amendments to commitments and leases
- Prepare memoranda and other reports on proposals, recommendations and other pertinent information on major modification requests for presentation to senior officers and the mortgage committee
- Receive and review all required pre-closing and post-closing documents

TYPES OF DECISIONS

- Negotiate changes in conditions and closing details with clients
- Approve, subject to final authorization, changes in certain business details (length of tenant leases, variances from certain construction requirements, etc.)
- Determine closing date that is most advantageous to the company's financial position
- Recommend acceptance of modifications to commitment terms
- Authorize the company's attorney to fund loans
- Interpret and review documentation for acceptability and conformance to business and legal requirements

CONSEQUENCES OF ERROR

- All statements or action taken are viewed as having the force of the company management approval behind them. Mishandling of negotiations or making ill-considered statements could lead to a lack of confidence and loss of credibility on the part of clients

ORGANIZATIONAL RELATIONSHIPS

- The incumbent reports to the mortgage officer in charge and/or the second vice president of mortgage and real estate

- No positions report to this position

WORK RELATIONSHIPS
- Work with borrowers, company attorneys, outside attorneys, servicers, developers, etc. on loan-closing details
- Consult and refer various documents to the company's production section, appraisal and engineering staffs, investment law staff, and the cash management division
- Report in writing and orally to the mortgage committee and supervising mortgage officers

EDUCATION AND EXPERIENCE
- No specific educational level is necessary
- At least one year's general business and/or related experience is required at the entry level

REPRESENTATIVE SKILLS AND KNOWLEDGE
- This position requires knowledge of various documentation and legal instruments (leases, construction reports, operating agreements, plans and specifications, appraisals, buy-sell arrangements, etc.)
- Have excellent verbal communication skills
- Be a strong negotiator

WORKING CAPITAL MANAGEMENT

General Credit Manager

Basic Function: Establish and administer the broad credit and collection policies of the company as they apply to domestic and export customer sales of the manufacturing divisions and specialized distribution and service units. This receivables management is carried out through all company credit and collection units on both a direct and non-direct basis as required to optimize the company's receivables turnover.

PRIMARY RESPONSIBILITIES AND DUTIES

- Approve all extraordinary lines of credit, including those that exceed delegated field authority
- Visit key customers to maintain good commercial relationships and determine financial liability
- Work with appropriate division and field sales personnel to coordinate and communicate terms of payment, credit decisions, and disputed or uncollectible billings
- Prepare monthly cash collection forecasts and monitor and report daily cash receipts
- Coordinate all legal matters pertaining to receivables management with company and outside attorneys
- Establish objectives for domestic and export treasury managers
- Supervise the maintenance and safekeeping of special customer records, files, reports, and ledgers
- Represent the company at financial professional association meetings and seminars
- Keep informed of legislation and changes in laws and regulations which affect financing, credit, and collection policies and procedures
- Sign documents as necessary as an authorized officer of the company
- Direct the preparation of periodic reports on receivables and analyze customer's accounts and reserve requirements; report unusual trends in developments to management along with corrective action needed
- Develop policy and procedures for recruiting and soliciting professional personnel to staff the credit and collection offices
- Administer the department salary program and provide for direct and indirect training of department personnel
- Supervise the effective utilization of funds allocated for the operations of domestic and export credit collection units
- Supervise the booking and collection processing of domestic and export customer's notes and trade acceptances
- Prepare and formulate, within prescribed time limits, various data and reports as may be required by the Vice President-Treasurer
- Develop budgets for domestic and export credit and collection units

Types of Decisions

- Final decision-making responsibility exists in credit/collection problems and procedures, personnel decisions, reporting unit structure, budget and merit increase considerations, and establishment of department/receivables objectives. (All major aspects of the preceding are reviewed with the Vice President-Treasurer.)
- Recommendations concerning bad debts are submitted to the Vice President-Treasurer for final approval
- Objectives are established for domestic and export credit and collection units

Organizational Relationships

- The incumbent directly supervises four zone treasury managers, three directors of treasury services, one subsidiary vice president and treasurer, one manager of international collections, and one credit manager of international standard sales. Approximately 150 employees report through these positions
- The incumbent reports directly to the Vice President-Treasurer

Work Relationships

- Work with marketing management to increase both domestic and export sales volume through financing plans designed to accomplish this goal with minimum risk
- Supervise the counseling of both domestic and export customers as to better financing arrangements and more effective control of internal operations
- Enhance the company's image among customers by providing appropriate credit and collection activities conducive to continuing and broadening the commercial relationships that exist

Education and Experience

- BS or BA required with a major in accounting or finance
- Should have five years minimum in direct handling of open account credit and secured transactions, ten years minimum of direct supervision of this type of activity in a management capacity, five years minimum as a zone, regional manager, or director of treasury services

Representative Skills and Knowledge

- Requires a working knowledge of corporate finance, banking, commercial finance, and international credit policies and procedures

Desired traits:
- A disciplined and determined negotiator
- A leader and motivator of people
- Skilled in selling programs and policies to customers and company units
- Objective in thinking and open to new ideas
- Able to size up a situation and act decisively
- Skilled in short and long-range planning and reorganization

Assistant Treasurer-Cash Control and Risk Management

Basic Function: Responsible for operations of the treasury department involving cash management operations with specific attention to the effective direction and control of corporate funds internally and through the company's various bank accounts.

PRIMARY RESPONSIBILITIES AND DUTIES
- Manage, in conjunction with lock box banks retained by company, the processing of over 120,000 customer payments daily
- Disbursement of all company funds, including payrolls, pensions, and vendor payments
- Direct the management staff to assure compliance with stated objectives and planning in order to assure the effectiveness of the organization
- Sign checks and review and approve various documents such as wire transfer confirmations and investment letters
- Meet with banks and their representatives
- Perform various assignments for senior management
- Also responsible for the risk management/insurance function

TYPES OF DECISIONS
- Personnel: disciplinary action, hire, fire, promote, and transfer
- Anything of significant impact on the budget
- Kinds of insurance coverage to purchase
- Approve all changes in operating procedures in all areas of this department

CONSEQUENCES OF ERROR
- Error in receipts ($20 million daily) or disbursements (slightly less) could be significant to stockholders and customers
- Error in insurance area may be catastrophic; i.e., failing to insure something resulting in a major loss

ORGANIZATIONAL RELATIONSHIPS
- The incumbent has authority over 25 subordinates
- Stated goals are reviewed on quarterly basis with supervisor

WORK RELATIONSHIPS
- Meet daily with the Treasurer to discuss current problems, answer his superiors' inquiries
- Also meet regularly with the Director-Risk Management, Manager-Cash Control and assistant managers and supervisors as needed

EDUCATION AND EXPERIENCE
- Minimum BA
- Formerly held positions as Director of Auditing, General Manager-Administration and Division Manager-Customer Service

REPRESENTATIVE SKILLS AND KNOWLEDGE
Should:
- Be familiar with cash control operations including bank operations such as check processing, lock box, and Federal Reserve check clearing operations
- Have knowledge of bank dispersing and other bank services

Must:
- Have a working knowledge of customer service activities such as billing, collections, and the business office's operations
- Possess the analytical skills to review financial statements and understand certain loss and reserve relationships
- Have the ability to communicate in all forms effectively
- Be creative and resourceful
- Be able to motivate personnel

Senior Banking Analyst

Basic Function: Assist the supervisor of financial services with short-term asset management and provide financial data and other services as requested by various departments.

PRIMARY RESPONSIBILITIES AND DUTIES
- Project short-term debt schedule for financing requirements
- Project the required compensating balances for bank services
- Research various financing possibilities regarding their economic advantages
- Plan shifts in cash balances to gain advantageous rates on investments or lower rates on borrowings
- Participate in arrangements with dealers and/or banks for short-term borrowings, roll overs or maturities
- Participate in arrangements with dealers and/or banks for short-term investments of company funds and funds of subsidiary companies
- Review the major parameters of all bank accounts maintained to relate the actual condition of the accounts to the objectives desired
- Monitor agent collection performance in handling coupons and funds
- Resolve minor problems developing in the various bank accounts
- Review requests for petty cash funds, recommend action, and monitor activity
- Prepare summary reports of the changing cash position and money market conditions
- Prepare reports highlighting current financial events
- Update listings of securities bought and sold during the period

TYPES OF DECISIONS
- Make predictions concerning future volume of services that may be requested from banks, the level of borrowings or investment by the company, etc. (These estimates are dependent upon bank policies and prices, consumer behavior and management decisions.)

- Decisions made impact bank accounts of $22 million, pension fund accounts of $150 million, interest calculations of $16 million, and other miscellaneous assets

Consequences of Error

- Because of the close working relationship necessary with multiple banks, inappropriate activities and/or conversations can significantly impair relationships and strategies necessary to achieve short-term asset management goals

Organizational Relationships

- The incumbent reports directly to the supervisor of financial services
- Long-term objectives are reviewed on a six-month basis; formal discussions are held frequently on short-term objectives
- Most reports require supervisor's signature
- General policies are occasionally reviewed and discussed to insure consistency
- No personnel are directly supervised

Work Relationships

- Work regularly with vice presidents and managers of 20 banks in three major metropolitan areas to resolve differences in bank statement balances and bank account analysis, interest calculations, etc.
- Work regularly with the vice presidents and trust managers of five large trustees in two major cities to resolve differences and report transactions for the pension fund
- Provide reports and statistics to the Office of the Treasury
- Audit payments to various trustees and study costs of trustees with the Director of Investor Relations
- Provide regular reports and information to the general accounting and auditing departments
- Discuss and resolve problems encountered in daily disbursements relating to the accounts payable department

Representative Skills and Knowledge

Must:
- Have a good working knowledge of accounting
- Have a good working knowledge of financial analysis
- Have a strong statistical background
- Be knowledgeable of, and understand, company practices

SECTION III

PERSPECTIVES ON EDUCATION

OPPORTUNITIES AND CHALLENGES

Source: American Assembly of Collegiate Schools of Business—The International Association for Management Education (AACSB), 600 Emerson Road, Suite 300, St. Louis, MO 63141-6762; phone: 314-872-8481; fax: 314-872-8495; Copyright © 1999; Web site: http://www.aacsb.edu. All rights reserved.

College and university faculty enjoy many work and lifestyle privileges that typically are not available in other walks of life. Significant professional and intellectual autonomy allows for an unusual degree of freedom in defining work arrangements and in developing areas of academic activity. Nine-month contracts frequently allow faculty the freedom to travel and undertake alternative teaching, research and consulting assignments, if they wish. The opportunity to teach highly motivated students, to undertake research and to develop satisfying professional relations with colleagues across the country and the world is without parallel in most other professions. Being a professor also means having the opportunity to search for knowledge and techniques that will improve the practice of management in ways that improve society and contribute to "the greater good." In short, it provides a chance to have an impact on individuals, as well as the larger society.

Faculty members at business schools often earn substantially higher salaries than faculty members in other academic fields. According to an annual survey conducted by the American Assembly of Collegiate Schools of Business (AACSB), the demand for Ph.Ds in business schools rose slightly this year according to results of the latest AACSB surveys of business doctoral production and faculty demand. The overall vacancy rate rose to 6.8 percent, compared to 6.6 percent a year ago. Planned growth in business faculty positions is up by one-half of a percentage point, from 3.1 percent last year to 3.6 percent this year. Combined with additional compensation for activities such as summer teaching and research activities, consulting assignments, executive program teaching, textbook writing, and sponsored papers and speeches, many business faculty enjoy very attractive incomes.

The demand for faculty in the business disciplines remains good though not as strong as in the recent past when there were up to three positions open for every doctoral graduate. Still, relative to other academic fields where the supply of new doctorates exceeds the number of positions available by a significant number, business doctorates continue to have a greater chance of obtaining an academic appointment. Other positive factors are options for taking a position in industry as a researcher, analyst or consultant. For example, an increasing number of companies have created their own executive education centers and employ some faculty full time. There also are increased opportunities at consulting firms that provide services to companies, such as strategic planning, human resource management assistance, economic forecasting, financial advice, marketing, and information systems design. Some companies maintain research and development units that include activities in one of the business disciplines.

Clearly, few careers today offer the rich intellectual and personal challenge, monetary reward and flexible life-style that are available to business school faculty members.

THE DYNAMICS OF MANAGEMENT EDUCATION

It is surprising perhaps to discover that many business school doctoral students have focused prior studies on seemingly unrelated academic fields, such as psychology, sociology, mathematics, statistics, computer science, physics, geography, or political science. Some students may never have taken a business class before entering a business doctoral program! This seeming paradox is understood more easily when the variety and complexity of issues typically addressed by business school teaching and research are considered. These topics range from the vastly complex international monetary system to the pricing of a computer chip; from an assessment of the effectiveness of different methods of managing and organizing large corporations to the nature of embryonic entrepreneurial ventures; from the theoretical analysis of financial portfolios to the art of managing an opera company; from the complex psychological aspects of consumer demand to the subtle skills of effectively coordinating interpersonal relationships in an elaborate organization; from managing intricate production processes to establishing and maintaining effective and efficient financial controls and information systems within organizations, both public and private. The globalization of markets and the necessity of developing knowledge that is relevant to contexts outside the U.S. impinge on teaching and research in business. New technologies, changing social and cultural contexts, and issues of social, political and ethical responsibility also must be embraced by business and management scholars. Taken together, these and other issues constitute an extensive body of knowledge that explains a sizeable part of our economic and social world and, in addition, yields skills and tools useful for everyday existence.

Faculty members are the most critical resource in any academic institution. Business faculty are experts on existing knowledge in their fields, they develop new knowledge and ideas through research and consulting, and they interpret and transmit knowledge through teaching and learning processes with students and professionals. The study of business and management takes place in a professional context that requires an interdisciplinary and applied orientation irrespective of the field of specialization. This distinguishes business schools from academic departments in the natural and social sciences where disciplinary purity is the norm. Professional education demands that the line between theory and practice be transparent and that it be crossed frequently. While intellectual rigor is critical, professional relevance is equally important. Business faculty members need to have their feet planted firmly in rigorous theory, as well as in applied business issues.

The work of business faculty has traditionally been organized around a set of specialized fields or disciplines such as accounting, finance, marketing, economics, organizational behavior, production and operations, management information systems, strategy, and business policy, etc. This specialized knowledge is critical to ensure intellectual rigor. Increasingly, however, the organization of business schools has moved in the direction of interdisciplinary and problem tissue-oriented teaching and research groups. Faculty seeks to strike a balance between loyalty to their specialized fields and the need to work with colleagues in a cross-disciplinary manner. This tension between specialization and interdisciplinary work is one factor that creates an exciting intellectual environment for business faculty. The primary differences between business school faculty and professors in other areas lie not in the nature of the basic disciplines and their theoretical foundations, but rather in the type of issues addressed, the potential for professional application, and the multi-disciplinary approaches to teaching and research.

CHOOSING A SCHOOL

Unlike undergraduate or master's-level education where individual courses and highly structured learning with many different faculty are the norm, doctoral education places a much greater emphasis on self-directed learning and close relationships with a few faculty in the area of specialization. Having one or two faculty "mentors" who work closely with the student to define a course of study, prepare for qualifying examinations, provide guidance through the disseriatim maze and assist with finding the first faculty position is critical to success. Given these conditions, it is especially important to select a doctoral program carefully.

How does a student choose from among so many schools? Personal considerations, including location and available doctoral offerings in a specialized field of interest, are criteria that may help narrow the range of possibilities. An obvious consideration is whether a particular school has faculty who specializes in the area of interest of the prospective student. Although it may seem obvious that this is an important criteria, many students assume that most schools offer similar types of specializations and pay relatively little attention to the specific research interests of faculty and their areas of expertise. This can cause some unpleasant surprises once a student begins a doctoral program. Even among the leading doctoral programs at renowned research universities, there are major differences in the areas in which they have national and international recognition for research and teaching. It pays to take the time to research the characteristics of faculty and their interest areas no matter what school you consider.

One way to obtain information on faculty and schools is to consult with faculty known to the student for help in defining an appropriate set of potential state, regional, or national programs. An additional source of information is to consult the key research journals to identify individual scholars who are doing research and writing articles in the field of interest. If feasible, it is beneficial to visit the campus to meet with appropriate doctoral program officials and faculty members with whom you are likely to work should you apply and be accepted to the program. This also is a good time to explore what teaching and research assistantships are available, since these activities will help frame relationships with faculty and provide important financial support.

The degree of selectivity in admissions of individual schools is another obvious factor to consider. Once a set of schools has been identified, it is appropriate to apply for admission to several doctoral programs that appear to meet specific interests. Once an applicant has been admitted to one or more institutions, it may be necessary to explore in greater detail the relative strengths of each school, given the individual's academic interests. There also may be other issues to consider. Such as financial assistance, opportunities for teaching and research experience, and the placement records of the institution. Asking a school for a placement record of recent doctoral graduates is especially important since this information can be helpful in projecting the kinds of employment opportunities likely to be available once doctoral studies have been completed.

Ph.D./DBA

The two principal degree designations offered by business doctoral programs are the Ph.D. (Doctor of Philosophy) and the DBA (Doctor of Business Administration). In an earlier era of management education, the DBA was popularly regarded as providing a more general exposure to business topics, while the Ph.D. was viewed as focusing more on research in a given business specialty. In practice, over the years the distinction between these degrees at many institutions has become blurred. At present, the Ph.D. is more widely available from business schools than the DBA. Investigation of specific doctoral programs will yield information on the particular orientation of the degree at respective schools.

Rankings/Accreditation

Studies that purport to rank business schools generally or business doctoral programs in particular, are occasionally published by some organizations and individuals. However, such rankings, at best, are highly subjective and depend on unscientific survey data, word-of-mouth and other "image" factors. Moreover, rankings by national business magazines often focus exclusively on MBA programs and there may be little correlation between MBA rankings and the quality of doctoral programs. Rankings cannot reflect the needs of individual students and should not be substituted for a student's own investigation of particular school characteristics.

Another factor to consider is accreditation. Basically, accreditation means that knowledgeable peers from other institutions have determined that a school's programs meet standards for faculty composition and development, curriculum content, instructional resources, students, intellectual contributions, all linked to its mission. Virtually all colleges and universities in the United States hold institution-with-accreditation conferred by regional accrediting agencies. Within the field of business and management, however, separate "specialized" accreditation is conferred in the United States by AACSB. As a practical matter, the growth of "diploma mills" that offer doctoral degrees in business and other fields has made it even more crucial that prospective students exercise special care in selecting a school. If a student is considering a doctoral program at a U.S. institution that does not hold AACSB accreditation, it is particularly important to obtain a complete placement record of that school's business doctoral graduates.

THE BENEFITS OF AN MBA: A COMPARISON OF GRADUATES AND NON-GRADUATES

By Mary Kay Dugan, William R. Grady, Betsy Payn, and Terry R. Johnson
Source: Graduate Management Admission Council (GMAC), 1750 Tyson Boulevard, Suite 1100, McLean, VA 22102; phone: 703-749-0131; fax: 703-749-0169; Copyright © 1999; Website: http:// www.gmac.org. All rights reserved.

Prospective students considering a graduate management education expect that it will give them some advantage in the marketplace. More specifically, they expect that a graduate management education will provide them with the specific skills they need to obtain a job that is both satisfying and financially rewarding. However, prospective students must weigh the anticipated benefits of attending a graduate management program against the potential costs of such a program. Since these costs can be substantial, involving not only tuition but potentially large opportunity costs as well, graduate management programs recognize that they can meet the expectations of their students only if graduates experience substantial positive career outcomes.

To date there have been very little quantifiable data about the career benefits of a graduate management degree. A common way to assess such benefits is to examine the starting salaries of graduates. Typically, a graduate management school tracks the salaries of its own graduates and compares the data to information reported by other schools. However, such a comparison doesn't really capture the benefits of a graduate management education.

To fully understand the net gains of the MBA, one must first determine the present value of those gains in earnings that are attributable to an individual's having attained the degree. The second step is to compare that value to the net present value of the full costs of completing an MBA program. Such an analysis requires complex multivariate modeling to control for the myriad of factors affecting the earnings of individuals over time. In addition, a full assessment of the value of the MBA must take into account multiple outcome measures besides earnings.

A comprehensive understanding of the value of the MBA degree is beyond the scope of this article. Here, we provide descriptive information that lays the groundwork for a more comprehensive analysis. In particular, we present information on employment outcomes for nationally representative samples of graduates and non-graduates. These comparisons are based on data from the GMAT Registrant Survey for graduates of various types of graduate management schools, as well as for individuals who were at one point interested enough in a management career to register for the GMAT, but who decided either not to pursue or not to complete the degree.

The Wave IV GMAT Registrant Survey provides a unique opportunity to examine the benefits of the MBA beyond an analysis of starting salaries. We use the survey data to compare the employment outcomes of MBAs with the outcomes of two groups of non-graduates: those who matriculated but never completed the degree, and those who never attended a management program.

The Wave IV data allow us to examine short-term employment outcomes for a nationally representative sample approximately seven years after registration for the GMAT.[1] Although there are many different ways of examining the benefits of the degree, in this article we present evidence from the GMAT Registrant Survey on the following three key dimensions measured at Wave IV: current earnings, management responsibility, and job satisfaction.

DATA

Wave IV of the GMAT Registrant Survey obtained considerable information about the current jobs of all respondents. The variables considered in this analysis include the respondent's earnings in the current job, whether or not the respondent has managerial responsibilities in the current position, and the respondent's level of satisfaction with present pay, work, and opportunities for promotion. Current earnings, as reported in this analysis, are adjusted to a full-time equivalent of earned annual income. Respondents who were not working at the time of the Wave IV survey, and who thus had no earned income, are also included in this analysis. The measure of management responsibilities is a dichotomous variable that indicates whether the respondent's current position includes managerial responsibilities.

Information regarding current job satisfaction was measured using three scales from the Job Descriptive Index.[2] The first scale measures satisfaction with pay and contains nine adjectives or short phrases describing current pay (e.g., *fair, barely live on income, well-paid*). The second scale measures satisfaction with work in the present job and contains eighteen adjectives or phrases (e.g., *fascinating, routine, satisfying, boring*). The third scale measures satisfaction with opportunities for promotion and contains nine adjectives or phrases (e.g., *good opportunities for promotion, infrequent promotions, and dead-end job*).

Respondents were asked to check "yes," "no," or "don't know" for each of the adjectives or phrases. Agreement with positive adjectives or phrases was given a score of 3, as was disagreement with negative phrases. Disagreement with positive phrases and agreement with negative phrases were given a score of 0. Responses "don't know" received a score of 1.[3] The scales measuring satisfaction with pay and opportunities for promotion range from 9 (complete dissatisfaction) to 27 (complete satisfaction), with scores above 9 indicating at least some level of satisfaction. The scale measuring satisfaction with work ranges from 0 (total dissatisfaction) to 54, total satisfaction, with scores above 18 indicating some satisfaction.

---

[1] The Wave I questionnaire was mailed to 7,006 individuals who registered to take the GMAT on one of the four test dates from June 1991 through March 1992. The Wave IV survey was sent out about eighty-seven months (or seven years) after the Wave I survey and was completed by 3,769 respondents. Data are weighted to account for non-response and for over-sampling of minorities such that the results are representative of the general registrant population.

[2] The Job Descriptive Index (JDI) was developed by Smith, Kendall, and Hulin, *The Measurement of Satisfaction in Work and Retirement: A Strategy for the Study of Attitudes* (Skokie, IL: Rand-McNally, 1969).

[3] Ibid.

We examine these outcomes for graduates and non-graduates of MBA programs. Graduates are divided into three categories, based on the competitiveness levels of the schools from which they graduated. In this way we can determine whether there are any differences among graduates by school competitiveness level. We compare these groups of graduates to two groups of non-graduates: those who matriculated in a graduate management program but left before completing the program, and those who never enrolled.

The measure of school competitiveness used in this analysis is based both on the number of applicants a school admits and on the distribution of GMAT scores in the score reports the school receives. That is, we used the number of admitted applicants to determine what the cutoff score for the school would be if admission decisions were based on the GMAT score alone. For example, if 100 applicants per year were admitted to a particular school, we would define the hundredth-highest GMAT score received by the school as the cutoff score. Although we recognize that admission decisions are based on more than GMAT performance alone, this cutoff score still provides a useful index of school competitiveness by showing the kinds of applicants a school is able to attract. For purposes of this article, schools have been divided into three categories: highly competitive (a GMAT cutoff score of 650 or above), competitive (a GMAT cutoff score ranging from 500 to 650), and less competitive (a GMAT cutoff score below 500).

The results in this article are based on Wave IV Registrant Survey respondents only. Analyses are presented separately by pace of graduate study (i.e., full-time versus part-time study), since full-time and part-time programs serve very different markets. We expect that employment outcomes may differ by pace of study, a factor that is defined differently for matriculants and non-matriculants. For matriculants, it is defined as the actual pace of study reported in the survey. This definition of pace is used both for those who graduated and those who enrolled but left before completing the degree. For those who never enrolled, pace of study is defined as the respondents' intended pace at the time of GMAT registration.

Respondents who were enrolled in a graduate management program at the time of the Wave IV survey and those individuals missing on pace of study are excluded from the analysis. Our sample includes 1,343 respondents who enrolled or intended to enroll in full-time programs, and 2,100 respondents who enrolled or intended to enroll in part-time programs.

FULL-TIME PROGRAMS

We begin our examination of the benefits of the MBA by comparing graduates of full-time programs to two groups of non-graduates. Our comparison is in terms of earnings, managerial responsibility, and satisfaction with the current job. We also compare outcomes of subgroups of graduates by school competitiveness level.

EARNINGS

A natural starting point for obtaining insights into the benefits of the MBA is to compare the annual earnings of graduates with the annual earnings of non-graduates. Figure 1 shows the median annual current earnings at Wave IV for three groups of graduates, stratified by school competitiveness level. The earnings data for these three groups were measured an average of four years after completion of the MBA degree. Also shown are median earnings for two groups of non-graduates: those who dropped out of their programs, and those who never enrolled.

As shown in this figure, graduates of highly competitive full-time programs have the highest annual earnings in their current jobs of any of the groups examined (with median earnings of approximately $96,000 annually). Overall, graduates have median earnings of $58,000 annually, which is considerably higher than the overall median of $45,000 for the two non-graduate groups. Graduates from the highly competitive and competitive programs have higher earnings than do either of the two non-MBA comparison groups. However, graduates of less competitive/unaccredited programs have annual earnings that are much more similar to the earnings of the two non-graduate groups.

Figure 1 also indicates that among the two non-graduate groups, registrants who enrolled in a graduate management program but who left before earning a degree have lower earnings than registrants who never enrolled. It may be that those who chose not to enroll in a graduate management program based that decision in part on an assessment of their earning potential without a graduate management degree. In addition, there may be differences in the composition of the groups (e.g., ability, gender, and race) that may account for some of the differences we found. It is also important to note that those who never enrolled are less likely to have had the career interruptions experienced by those who left the work force to enroll in full-time programs.

MANAGERIAL RESPONSIBILITY

Next, we examine whether graduates at Wave IV are any more likely than non-graduates to be in management positions. The results of our analysis are shown in Figure 2. As a group, graduates of full-time programs are significantly more likely than the members of the two non-graduate groups to report having management responsibilities in their current jobs. However, graduates of less competitive/unaccredited programs appear to have the same degree of likelihood as those in the two non-graduate groups to report management responsibilities. In contrast, graduates of highly competitive full-time programs are much more likely than those in any other group to indicate that they function as managers in their current jobs. Our results show that the more competitive the school attended, the more likely it is for a graduate to be in a management position at Wave IV.

Job Satisfaction

In this section we examine job satisfaction with respect to pay, work done in the present job, and opportunities for promotion. We begin by looking at satisfaction

Figure 1. Median Earnings at Wave IV: Full-Time Programs

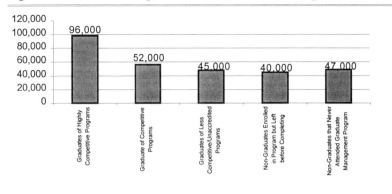

Figure 2. Percentages of Respondents with Managerial Responsibilities: Full-Time Programs

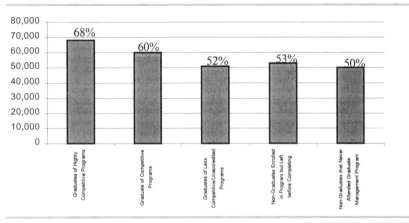

with pay. Figure **3** shows the mean job-satisfaction ratings and pay for graduates of full-time programs and for two groups of non-graduates. Scores on the pay-satisfaction scale range from 0 to 27, with scores above 9 indicating some level of satisfaction with pay. As shown, all groups report mean scores far above 9, indicating a fairly high level of satisfaction with pay. In addition, for the most part there are very few differences in the mean scores of graduates and non-graduates. Although graduates as a group are more likely to be satisfied with pay than are non-graduates, these differences are small. Moreover, even though graduates of the most competitive full-time programs have significantly higher median earnings than do members of the other groups, they report only very slightly higher levels of satisfaction with pay. It appears that satisfaction with pay may be relative to expectations.

The Wave IV GMAT Registrant Survey also obtained information on satisfaction with the work performed in the present job. Scores on this scale range from 0 to 54, with scores above 18 indicating some level of satisfaction. Figure **4** shows the mean

Figure 3. Mean Job-Satisfaction Rating with Respect to Present Pay: Full-Time Programs

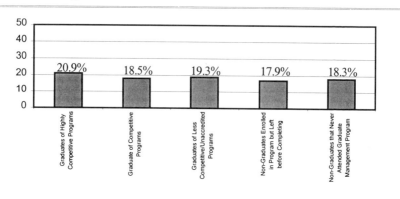

job-satisfaction ratings for graduates of full-time programs (by school competitiveness level) and for the two groups of non-graduates. Similar to the results described above for pay, those in all groups report fairly high and very similar levels of satisfaction with the work they perform in their current jobs. These results indicate that despite the fact that graduates—particularly graduates of the most competitive full-time programs—are significantly more likely to report that they are currently managers, their level of satisfaction with the work they do is very similar to that of non-graduates.

Finally, we examine satisfaction with opportunities for promotion. Scores on this scale range from 0 to 27, with scores above 9 indicating some level of satisfaction. As shown in Figure 5, while all groups report satisfaction with opportunities for promotion, there is considerable variation in the mean levels of satisfaction for graduate and non-graduate groups. In contrast to the two previous measures of satisfaction, graduates as a whole are significantly more satisfied with their opportunities for promotion than are members of the two non-graduate groups. Furthermore, graduates of the most highly competitive graduate programs are significantly more likely than graduates of less competitive programs to be satisfied with opportunities for promotion. Finally, graduates of less competitive/unaccredited programs report slightly lower levels of satisfaction with opportunities for promotion than do members of either non-graduate group.

Part-Time Programs

We turn now to an examination of those who chose part-time graduate programs, comparing the results for graduates of part-time programs with the results for two groups of non-graduates. We also compare the employment outcomes of graduates of highly competitive part-time programs with those of graduates of competitive and less competitive programs with respect to earnings, managerial responsibility,

Figure 4. Mean Job-Satisfaction Rating for Work in Present Job: Full-Time Programs

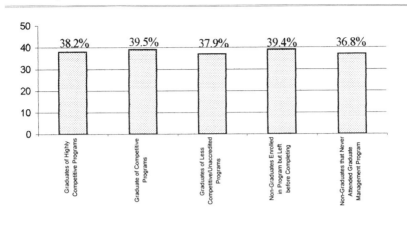

Figure 5. Mean Job-Satisfaction Rating with Respect to Promotion Opportunities: Full-Time Programs

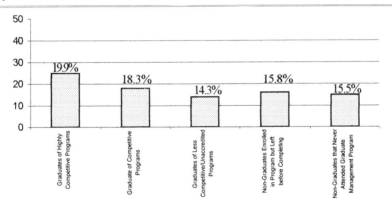

and satisfaction with the current job.

Earnings

As shown in Figure **6**, graduates of the most highly competitive part-time programs have the highest earned annual incomes in their current jobs of any of the groups examined. Specifically, median earnings of graduates of highly competitive programs are approximately $80,000 annually. Overall, graduates of part-time programs have a median salary of $57,000. This is considerably higher than the overall median of $50,000 for those in the two non-graduate groups, and it is similar to the overall

Figure 6. Median Earnings at Wave IV: Part-Time Programs

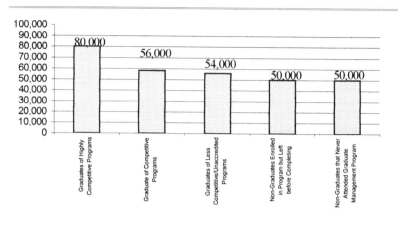

median earnings for graduates of full-time programs ($58,000 annually) reported earlier.

Managerial Responsibility

We also examined whether graduates of part-time programs are any more likely than non-graduates to report being in management positions at Wave IV. Overall, the results presented in Figure 7 show that graduates of part-time programs are significantly more likely than those in the two non-graduate groups to report having managerial responsibilities. However, unlike the results found for graduates of full-time programs, among graduates of part-time programs there are no significant differences by competitiveness level in the likelihood of having managerial duties at Wave IV.

Job Satisfaction

Figure 8 shows differences in the mean job-satisfaction level with respect to pay for graduates of part-time programs (by school competitiveness level) and for two groups of non-graduates. As described above, scores on this scale range from 0 to 27, with values above 9 indicating some level of satisfaction. Similar to the results of our analysis of full-time graduate programs, members of all part-time groups had mean scores well above 9, indicating a very high level of satisfaction with pay. In addition, there are only very small differences between the mean satisfaction scores of graduates and non-graduates.

Again similar to the findings for graduates of full-time programs, graduates of the most competitive part-time programs report only slightly higher levels of satisfaction with their pay, despite having significantly higher earnings than the other graduate groups. It is interesting to note that the mean satisfaction levels for all of the part-time groups shown here are higher than those for the comparable full-time groups (see Figure 3), even though the median earnings of the full-time groups are higher.

Figure 7. Percentages of Respondents with Managerial Responsibilities: Part-Time Programs

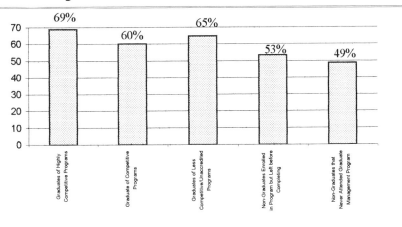

Figure 8. Mean Job-Satisfaction Rating with Respect to Present Pay: Part-Time Programs

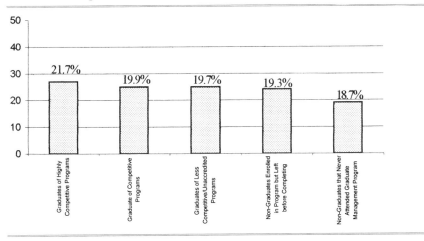

We next compare the mean job-satisfaction levels with work for graduates of part-time programs and two groups of non-graduates. Similar to the results for full-time programs, the results shown in Figure 9 indicate that all of the part-time groups have fairly high and very similar levels of satisfaction with work. Thus, in terms of satisfaction with pay and with the work performed, there are no large differences between graduates of part-time programs and members of the two non-graduate comparison groups.

Finally, we look at satisfaction with opportunities for promotion. As shown in Figure 10, similar to all other measures of satisfaction, all groups had mean scores surpassing minimal satisfaction levels. However, graduates overall reported higher

Figure 9. Mean Job-Satisfaction Rating for Work in Present Job: Part-Time Programs

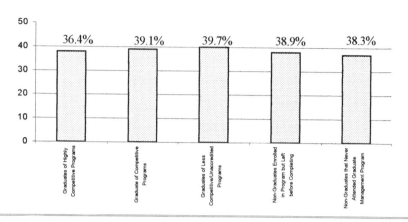

Figure 10. Mean Job-Satisfaction Rating with Respect to Promotion Opportunities: Part-Time Programs

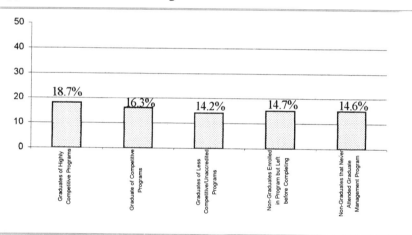

levels of satisfaction with opportunities for promotion than did non-graduates. It appears that this difference is driven by graduates of highly competitive and competitive part-time programs. Graduates of less competitive/unaccredited programs are more similar to members of the two non-graduate groups. It is interesting to note that the mean satisfaction levels for all of the part-time groups shown here are lower than the levels found for the comparable full-time groups (see Figure 5).

Summary and Discussion

The results presented in this article provide important insights into the short-term benefits of obtaining a graduate management degree. Overall, graduates of both full-time and part-time programs fare significantly better than non-graduates in terms of earnings, management responsibility, and satisfaction with opportunities for promotion. Much of this advantage relative to non-graduates is driven by the fact that graduates of the most highly competitive program report more favorable employment outcomes. This finding is not surprising; one would expect greater gains for members of this group, who were selected by their programs on the basis of their much higher than average capabilities and credentials.

However, what is somewhat surprising is that graduates of the most highly competitive programs report levels of satisfaction with pay and work in their current jobs that are very similar to those both of other groups of graduates and of non-graduates. This finding holds despite the fact that graduates of the most highly competitive programs have higher earnings, greater management responsibility, and significantly higher levels of satisfaction with promotional opportunities. It may be that job satisfaction is relative to the varying expectations of the different groups.

We also found that graduates of the less competitive/unaccredited full-time and part-time programs report employment outcomes that are very similar to and, in some cases, somewhat less favorable than those of the non-graduates surveyed. Graduates in this group might be the least capable of all of the graduate groups and may, in fact, have the most to gain from attending a graduate management program. In addition, since the two non-graduate groups have not been divided based on some level of ability or on any hypothetical competitiveness of their applications, they are really not comparable to any single group of graduates defined on the basis of school competitiveness. As noted earlier, to fully understand the benefits of the MBA degree one would need to conduct additional analyses, taking potential compositional differences into account.

It is interesting to note that the two non-graduate groups in both the full-time and part-time analyses are very similar on the three outcomes examined, despite the fact that one group matriculated and the other did not. This finding appears to suggest that there are no added advantages to enrolling without completing a degree, since the outcomes for those who did and did not matriculate in a graduate management program are similar. One possible explanation is that the gains of an MBA are available only to graduates. However, it is quite possible that there may be some gains for matriculants that are not measured here. In addition, without adequately controlling for the compositional differences between these two groups, it is difficult to pinpoint why they are so similar.

The results reported here represent some very preliminary insights into the benefits of a graduate management education. We have provided some descriptive evidence that those who complete a graduate management program have greater value in the marketplace than non-graduates. Graduates can expect higher earnings, more responsible positions, and greater satisfaction with opportunities for promotion than non-graduates. Further, graduates' levels of satisfaction with pay and work are equal to or greater than those of non-graduates.

We caution that our analysis is based on short-term employment outcomes measured at Wave IV, roughly four years after graduation. We expect that the advantages of completing a graduate management degree may continue to increase over time, as graduates progress further in their careers. Furthermore, we have examined only a small subset of the possible advantages that a graduate management degree may provide graduates. There are many other potential gains to the degree not considered here. For example, while in school, graduates may have gained connections that led to better jobs. A more comprehensive understanding of the value of a graduate management degree requires further research to fully account for the benefits of the degree to graduates over time.

SECTION IV

CERTIFICATIONS AND DESIGNATIONS

CERTIFIED CASH MANAGER (CCM)

The sponsor. The Treasury Management Association (TMA) is the largest individual membership association representing those in the treasury and related financial professions. With members whose titles range from Analyst, Assistant Cash Manager and Accountant up to CFO, Treasurer, and Controller, TMA represents the spectrum of professionals in financial occupations. To support those members whose primary responsibilities are in cash management, TMA sponsors the Certified Cash Manager (CCM) credential.

The exam. The CCM is a test-based credential, being earned by passing a 200-question multiple-choice test which is based on a common body of knowledge contained in TMA's Essentials of Cash Management. Essentials of Cash Management is revised every three years by professional financial editors who are supervised by a committee of volunteers from the profession who practice treasury management and who hold the CCM. A separate task force of volunteers, all CCMs, writes a pool of questions, from which are drawn the 200 questions for the exam.

The body of knowledge. Essentials of Cash Management covers sixteen areas of cash and treasury management, including traditional areas of collections & disbursements, receivables & payables, corporate finance, and financial institution relationship management. Also included are short-term portfolio management, global treasury management, information & technology management, risk management, and electronic commerce.

Eligibility. Qualification to take the exam is determined according to one of two criteria. First, any applicant with two or more years of experience in treasury and/or cash management, or a graduate degree in business and one year of experience, is eligible to take the exam. This definition is intentionally broad and includes those who teach finance and/or accounting as well as those who provide services to the treasury profession, such as bankers.

CCM-Associate Program. The second route to taking the exam is to successfully complete a finance course, undergraduate or graduate, based on the content of Essentials of Cash Management. Upon graduation those individuals become eligible to take the CCM exam at its first offering. Those who pass are classified as CCM-Associates and given five years to attain the two years of experience. Once the experience component is met the "Associate" is dropped from the credential. Currently over thirty colleges and universities have registered their CCM-Associate programs with TMA.

Web site. For more information about TMA, please check out our web site: http://www.tma-net.org.

Contact. For further information about the CCM credential, contact :
Certification Department
Treasury Management Association
7315 Wisconsin Ave. Suite 600W
Bethesda, MD 20814
Telephone: (301) 907-2862

THE VALUE OF HAVING A CERTIFIED CASH MANAGER (CCM)

Aaron L. Phillips, D.B.A., CCM
Former Managing Director, Research & Information Services
Treasury Management Association

Many accountants, bankers, and cash managers have at least one thing in common: they pursue the Certified Cash Manager (CCM) credential sponsored by the Treasury Management Association (TMA). Collectively, over thirteen thousand individuals have attained the CCM since it was first offered in 1986. Annually, over two thousand individuals now register to take the CCM exam.

The CCM is an exam-based credential, based on a body of knowledge called *Essentials of Cash Management*, 6th edition. This book is published by TMA and is updated every three years by professional financial editors working with a committee of volunteers, each of whom has the CCM. The content of Essentials of Cash Management spans sixteen areas:

- The Role of Cash Management in Corporate Finance
- Accounting and Financial Concepts
- The U.S. Financial Environment
- Payments Systems
- Credits and Accounts Receivable Management
- Collections
- Cash Concentration
- Accounts Payable and Disbursements
- Electronic Commerce
- Information and Technology management
- Forecasting Cash Flows
- Short-Term Investments
- Borrowing
- Financial Risk Management
- International Cash Management
- Relationship Management

These sixteen areas for the CCM span the job responsibilities someone two years into the profession is expected to know. It is particularly relevant to college undergraduates since many of their early career employment opportunities lie in cash management.

In most finance-related occupations there are credentials which practitioners can pursue. In all but a few instances, a professional certification is not mandatory for employment. There exist, however, both tangible and intangible benefits to having a CCM, or, for that matter, one of many other business-related credentials.

Among the intangible benefits of holding a CCM is the acknowledgement that you have mastered a standardized body of knowledge. Since the CCM, like most other credentials, also has a continuing professional education component, it also says you are keeping up with the profession as it evolves.

Another intangible benefit of holding the CCM is very relevant to those entering the banking profession. Banks are among the leading providers of treasury management services. Those services include services such as lines of credit, wire transfers, zero balance checking accounts, controlled disbursement, check clearing, and account analysis. When a bank's relationship officer calls on a new client, an important element of that initial meeting is whether or not there is an understanding of the client's business and needs. The CCM says to the prospective customer "I know your business and the types of products you need to do your job."

On the tangible benefit side, companies reward individuals passing the exam with a bonus or pay raise. In addition, on a recent compensation survey TMA conducted, over half of the respondents indicated that a professional credential, particularly the CCM, improves their upward mobility.

CERTIFIED IN FINANCIAL MANAGEMENT (CFM)

The Certified Financial Management (CFM) designation requires candidates to have at least a bachelor's degree in any area from an accredited college or university, or achieve a satisfactory score on the Graduate Record Examination or the Graduate Management Admission Test, or hold a professional qualification comparable to the Certified Public Accountant; to pass all four parts of a comprehensive examination; and, to complete two years of professional experience in management accounting and/or financial management prior to, or within, seven years of having passed the examination. Examination material covers economics and corporate finance, organizational behavior, financial statement analysis, risk management, management reporting and analysis, decision analysis, capital budgeting, information systems, and management controls.

Certified in Management Accounting (CMA)

The Certified Management Accounting (CMA) designation requires candidates to have at least a bachelor's degree in any area from an accredited college or university, or achieve a satisfactory score on the Graduate Record Examination or the Graduate Management Admission Test, or hold a professional qualification comparable to the Certified Public Accountant; to pass all four parts of a comprehensive examination; and, to complete two years of professional experience in management accounting and/or financial management prior to, or within, seven years of having passed the examination. Examination material covers economics and corporate finance, organizational behavior, financial accounting and reporting, auditing, management reporting and analysis, decision analysis, capital budgeting, information systems, and management controls.

For additional information on the CMA and CFM programs contact:

Institute of Management Accounting
10 Paragon Drive
Montvale, NJ 07645-1760
Telephone: (800) 638-4427
www.imanet.org

Certified Public Accountant (CPA)

To become a Certified Public Accountant (CPA), you need to meet the requirements of the state of jurisdiction in which you wish to practice. These requirements, which vary from state to state, are established by law and administered by the state boards of accountancy.

To qualify for certification, you must:

- Complete a program of study in accounting at a college/university (the AICPA recommends at least 150 semester hours of college study to obtain the common body of knowledge for becoming a CPA; many states have passed legislation/regulation requiring 150 hours of education in order to be eligible to take the CPA exam);
- Pass the Uniform CPA Examination, which is developed and graded by the AICPA; and
- Have a certain amount of professional work experience in public accounting (not all states require this).

The Uniform CPA Examination is given over a two-day period twice annually (in May and November). The exam consists of four sections: Business Law & Professional Responsibilities; Auditing; Accounting & Reporting-Taxation, Managerial, and Governmental and Not-for-Profit Organizations; and Financial Accounting & Reporting-Business Enterprises. Once you have become a CPA, most states require you to take specified amounts of continuing professional education courses annually to retain your professional license to practice.

For more information about the CPA Exam, please contact:
American Institute of Certified Public Accountants
1211 Avenue of the Americas
New York, NY 10036
Telephone: (212) 596-2000
www.aicap.org

CHARTERED FINANCIAL ANALYST DESIGNATION (CFA)

The Chartered Financial Analyst (CFA) Program is a practical, applied, generalist program designed for investment professionals. Candidates must have a bachelor's degree or equivalent, pass a sequence of three comprehensive examinations of six hours each, have at least three years of experience related to the investment decision-making process, and abide by the Code of Ethics and Standards of Professional Conduct. The program covers ethical and professional standards, quantitative methods, economics, financial statement analysis and corporate finance, global markets and instruments, analysis of debt investments, analysis of equity investments, analysis of alternative investments, and portfolio management. Scholarships for both faculty and students are available.

For more information on the CFA Program, please contact:

Association for Investment Management and Research (AIMR)
Information Central
5 Boar's Head Lane
P.O. Box 3668
Charlottesville, VA 22903-0668
Telephone: (800) 247-8132
            (804) 980-3668
Internet: www.aimr.org
E-mail: info@aimr.org

INSURANCE CERTIFICATIONS

The two primary professional designations available to members of the insurance profession are the Chartered Life Underwriter (CLU) and the Chartered Property Casualty Underwriter (CPCU). Both require the successful completion of ten national examinations and meeting specific ethical and experience requirements. Preparation for the exams may be done through classes, study groups or individual study.

For more information contact:

The American Institute for Chartered Property Underwriters (AICPCU)
P.O. Box 3016
Malvern, PA 19355-0716
Telephone: (610) 644-2100
                      (800) 644-2101
www.aicpcu.org
Licensing requirements vary from state to state.

REAL ESTATE CERTIFICATIONS

Several professional designations are available to individuals pursuing a career in real estate. The National Association of Realtors (NAR), the dominant trade organization in the real estate field, and its several affiliated institutes and societies offer a variety of educational and training programs which, upon successful completion, can lead to professional designations in brokerage. (Residential, commercial, industrial and farmland) brokerage management international real estate, appraisal, property management, and counseling.

For more information, contact:

National Association of Realtors
430 North Michigan Avenue
Chicago, IL 60611
 Telephone: (312) 329-8200.
www.realtor.com/
nar.realtor.com/

Notes

Notes

Notes